#Share

#Share

Building Social Media Word of Mouth

Natalie T. Wood and Caroline K. Muñoz

#Share: Building Social Media Word of Mouth

Copyright © Business Expert Press, LLC, 2023.

Cover design by Charlene Kronstedt

Interior design by Exeter Premedia Services Private Ltd., Chennai, India

All rights reserved. No part of this publication may be reproduced, stored in a retrieval system, or transmitted in any form or by any means—electronic, mechanical, photocopy, recording, or any other except for brief quotations, not to exceed 400 words, without the prior permission of the publisher.

First published in 2022 by
Business Expert Press, LLC
222 East 46th Street, New York, NY 10017
www.businessexpertpress.com

ISBN-13: 978-1-63742-414-8 (paperback)
ISBN-13: 978-1-63742-415-5 (e-book)

Business Expert Press Digital and Social Media Marketing and Advertising Collection

First edition: 2022

10 9 8 7 6 5 4 3 2 1

To Conor, Ronan, and Ava,
who remind me that life is a journey, not a race.

To Jose, Max, and Sebastian
Thanks for your patience.

Description

Each day, millions of consumers venture online to search and exchange product information, seek out, and share opinions.

Electronic word-of-mouth (eWOM) communication has been shown to influence consumer actions across a variety of industries. A significant portion of eWOM occurs on social media platforms. Social word of mouth (sWOM)—a subset of eWOM—has incredible reach with the potential to influence over 4.6 billion active social media consumers.

The purpose of this book is to examine the influence of sWOM and provide guidance on how to operationalize its growing power. Our goal in writing this book is to bring together industry best practices and academic research to help you construct social media content that

- speaks with your brand voice,
- stimulates engagement,
- inspires consumers to #share,
- and complies with industry and federal guidelines.

Keywords

brand advocates; brand ambassadors; consumer reviews; eWOM; endorsers; Facebook; influencers; Instagram; Pinterest; regulations; social influence; social media marketing; social media policy; sWOM; Twitter; viral marketing; WOMM; word of mouth marketing; YouTube

Contents

Preface xi

Chapter 1	Social Word of Mouth Marketing (sWOM)	1
Chapter 2	The Social Consumer	29
Chapter 3	Social Business	53
Chapter 4	Storytelling	83
Chapter 5	Social Influencers and Employee Advocates	121
Chapter 6	The Power of Persuasion	141
Chapter 7	Legal and Regulatory Issues	155

About the Authors 199
Index 201

Preface

Social media is, in many ways, akin to the wild, Wild West—lawless, crazy, messy, and sometimes, a little brutal. If you agree, feel some sympathy for us who attempt to teach this topic. Without question, social media is a fascinating subject, and let's face it, it's not going anywhere. So, let's take the horse by the reigns, follow the regulatory laws, develop some order, and learn more about how you can use social media in your company. But, before we get carried away, we should warn you—this book is not a "Complete Guide to Social Media" (there are plenty of books that have tackled that monster). This book focuses on what lies at both the heart and soul of social media: what motivates consumers to update their Facebook status, retweet an exciting piece of news, and pin things they will probably never make (Hello, Bourbon Brown Sugar Maple Bacon Candy!). This book focuses on an underrepresented topic of digital and physical bookshelves. This book focuses on the subject of social sharing (#Share).

Everyday, consumers are drawn to social media to share their opinions, ideas, purchases, events, recent finds, and much more with their social networks. They also use social media to find information to help them make their purchase decisions. Logically, companies are drawn to social media to reach and engage with their consumers. However, engaging with consumers on social media is exceptionally challenging for many companies. The sheer volume of tweets, status updates, pins, and videos that consumers are exposed to every day is staggering—it is like drinking from a fire hose. Companies are increasingly frustrated that their social media efforts produce little results. It is not easy getting people to like your Facebook page, retweet your news alert, and comment on your video, and it is even more challenging to get them to discuss and share your posts with others.

When consumers share, they engage in word of mouth (WOM). One form of WOM is electronic WOM (eWOM). A wealth of books and websites discuss the importance of eWOM and how to use it for business purposes. Yet, there are limited resources on social WOM (sWOM). Certainly, there are similarities between eWOM and sWOM; however, we suggest that we should view sWOM as a subset of eWOM. We believe that there are differences—differences that warrant a closer look. And that is what we aim to do.

In this book, we discuss the importance of understanding the social consumer—who he or she is, what social media accounts he or she uses, why he or she uses them, what content he or she wants to engage with, and more importantly, what makes him or her want to share his or her opinion and your company message with others. We advocate that to be successful in engaging consumers in sWOM, it needs to be a companywide effort. Your company needs to become a social business where communicating and sharing on social media is a part of your company's DNA. Going back to our Wild West analogy, we highlight the various federal and industry regulations supporting sWOM and discuss the importance of developing a social media policy. We delve into how to create content that resonates with your consumers—content that engages them and that they feel compelled to discuss and share. We examine how to craft engaging textual stories and highlight the power of visuals. We also discuss how you can harness the powers of persuasion to encourage your consumers to share, retweet, comment, and like. Throughout, we offer examples of companies succeeding in this area and provide you with resources to help your company grow.

CHAPTER 1

Social Word of Mouth Marketing (sWOM)

Figure 1.1 *An example of social sharing on Twitter*
Source: Courtesy of C. Munoz.

Too personal? A tweet can say a lot. And a tweet with a hashtag and an image not only communicates more but is also much more likely to be shared. The screenshot in Figure 1.1 embodies many topics that this book will explore: the role of storytelling, the persuasive power of images, emotional appeals, personalization, and social sharing. It also marks the beginning of a positive story—which is where all good social media campaigns (and books) should begin.

In the summer of 2014, Coca-Cola launched the personalized "Share a Coke" campaign in the United States. Twenty oz. bottles of Coca-Cola, Diet Coke, and Coke Zero were adorned with 250 of the most popular American names for millennials and teens. Consumers were prompted to share their photos of the personalized bottles using #Shareacoke on social media. They could visit shareacoke.com to create and share virtual, personalized bottles on Instagram, Facebook, Tumblr, and Twitter. They could also be featured on Coke billboards by using #Shareacoke (Hitz 2014). Consumers were drawn to soda bottles that were emblazoned with not only their name but also the names of their family and friends. Coca-Cola's bottle personalization was putting into action something that Dale Carnegie taught us long before—"A person's name is to that person, the sweetest, most important sound in any language." So, naturally, consumers wanted to share their name discovery on Twitter, Facebook, and Instagram.

Over the course of the campaign, consumers shared their experiences via the #Shareacoke hashtag over 250,000 times (Deye 2015). During the 2014 campaign cycle, more than 353,000 bottles were disseminated virtually (Tadena 2014). Geo-tagging and sales were correlated, and sure enough, there was a significant relationship between social sharing and sales (Deye 2015). By all accounts, the initial campaign was a sales success; Coke saw sales growth of more than 30 percent in one week (Deye 2015). Further evidence of the campaign's success can also be found in its variations. In 2016, Coca-Cola launched "Share a Coke and a Song" which included song lyrics on labels, and in 2017, they printed holiday destinations on bottles distributed in the UK. More recently and with a focus on the COVID-19 pandemic, Coco-Cola created the "Holiday Heroes" Share a Coke campaign. Approximately, 40 heroes, such as caregiver, educator, and doctor, were placed on Coke labels (Arthur 2020). Today (or at least in 2022) you can still customize and purchase an 8 oz. Coca-Cola glass bottle for $6.00 (Coca-Cola 2022). Personalization is at the heart of why the Share a Coke campaign worked; however, part of their success was certainly attributed to the power of social word of mouth (sWOM) marketing.

> 93 percent of global consumers trust brand recommendations from family and friends more than any other forms of advertising. (Austin 2020)

Why Word of Mouth Marketing?

You are reading this book because you get it. Word of mouth (WOM) marketing is powerful—it impacts not only product preferences and purchasing decisions, but it serves to mold consumer expectations and even postpurchase product attitudes (Kimmel and Kitchen 2014). The beauty of branded WOM marketing communication is that it is a natural, normal part of our everyday conversations. In fact, over 2.4 billion conversations each day involve brands (Google; KellerFay Group 2016). The ample number of conversations related to products and services is attributable to the fact that we need and actively seek out input from family, friends, and even virtual strangers before we make a purchase. A 2021 study found that 98 percent of consumers surveyed believed that reviews were an "essential resource when making purchase decisions" (Power Reviews 2021). One of the reasons that family and friends' recommendations matter so much is that they are simply trusted more—92 percent of consumers worldwide trust recommendations from family and friends more than any other type of advertising (Nielsen 2012; Austin 2020).

Marketing executives (64 percent surveyed) agree that WOM marketing is the most effective type of marketing (Whitler 2014). Further evidence of the effectiveness and popularity of WOM marketing can be found in the growing influencer marketing industry. In fact, influencer marketing spending is predicted to be over $37 billion in 2024 (ANA 2020). Outside of an implicit understanding that people seem to prefer the opinions of others over a TV advertisement, billboard, or branded website, on what information are marketers basing these beliefs? Can we quantify the effect of WOM?

In 2014, WOMMA (now merged with the Association of National Advertisers (ANA)) along with six major brands commissioned a study to determine the return on investment (ROI) on WOM marketing (WOMMA 2014). This was the first major study addressing not only the differing category impact of WOM but also its role in the overall marketing mix. Not surprisingly, the results reinforce many established beliefs about WOM's level of importance.

- $6 trillion of annual consumer spending is driven by word of mouth (i.e., on an average 13 percent of consumer sales).
- WOM's impact on sales is greater for products that consumers are more involved with (i.e., more expensive, higher risk).

- Most of the impact of WOM (two-thirds) is through offline conversations, whereas one-third is through online WOM.
- WOM, directly and indirectly, impacts business performance. For example, it can drive traffic to website or search engines, which can then impact performance measures.
- WOM can amplify paid media (e.g., advertising) by as much as 15 percent. The value of one offline WOM impression can be 5–200 times more effective than a paid advertising impression.
- Two weeks after exposure, online WOM (85–95 percent) has a quicker impact than offline WOM (65–80 percent) and traditional media—TV (30–60 percent).

Are these numbers compelling enough?

If you were paying attention, you would have noticed that according to these statistics, offline WOM appears to matter much more. Wharton Professor and author of *Contagious,* Jonah Berger, also suggests that we are spending too much time and effort on looking at online WOM (Berger 2013). Research supports Berger's statement—a 2011 study from the Keller Fay Group found that only 7 percent of all brand-related WOM conversations occur online (Belicove 2011), with 94 percent of brand impressions happening offline (Google; KellerFay Group 2016). Berger suggests that this overestimation of online WOM occurs because we can easily see the conversation and we spend a lot of time online. And, we do spend a lot of time online; global online users spend approximately 7 hours per day online with roughly two-and-a-half hours spend on social media (We Are Social and Hootsuite 2022). In the United States, 85 percent of consumers are online every day, 48 percent are on the Internet multiple times a day, and 31 percent reporting an almost "constant" online presence (Perrin and Atske 2021). Without question, offline brand-related WOM matters more. But is online brand-related WOM limited to only 7 percent?

The truth is offline and online WOM are not like oil and water; they can and do mix. The WOMMA study illustrates that offline and online work together to, directly and indirectly, impact business performance. Consumers today move seamlessly between online and offline communication, making it increasingly difficult for us to pinpoint whether the message that we saw came to us in-person or via social media. And, the 7 percent?—that is, from a study completed in 2011 (aka 77 years ago in Internet dog years). To offer some perspective, in September 2011, Snapchat launched and Instagram only had 10 million users. Smartphone adoption of American adults was at 35 percent (Smith 2011). Things are different in 2022. Instagram now boasts approximately 1.5 billion registered users (We Are Social and Hootsuite 2022) and smartphone adoption is at 85 percent (Pew Research Center 2021).

Socializing online is seamlessly integrated into our offline lives. For today's consumers, particularly those from a younger generation, there is no offline or online socializing, it is simply socializing. Even when we are supposedly offline, we are drawn back through a symphony of chirps and beeps alerting us to an online conversation we should be responding to. We are being normalized to believe that we should upload images of our food, family outings, and post about positive and negative consumer experiences. Consumer e-commerce websites, such as Amazon, are providing more opportunities for not only consumer comments but also allowing individuals to upload images and videos showcasing their recent purchase. Consumer feedback or input is essential in the purchase of the product. This feedback is becoming increasingly visual; take for instance, the online rental dress company—Rent the Runway. On the primary product screen for each dress, Rent the Runway shares photographs taken by their consumers wearing the rented dress. The company encourages consumers to review the dress and provide personal information such as their height, weight, bust, body type, age, size worn, usual size, and event occasion. For any one dress, there could be over 100 photos highlighting not only the fit but "how others wore it," illustrating how to accessorize and wear one's hair with the dress.

With the advent and ubiquity of smartphones, image and video creation is easy and uploading almost instantaneous. In 2020, it was estimated that 3.2 billion photos and 720,000 hours of video were produced and shared each day (Thomson, Angus, and Dootson 2020). And if we break this down to the minute (in 2020), TikTok users watch 167 million videos, Instagram users share 65,000 photos, YouTube users stream 694,000 hours, and 2 million Snapchats are sent (Domo 2021).

Marketers also seek to further blend online and offline worlds. Television and print ads are prompting consumers to go online and watch, follow, and like. Traditional televised news programs routinely integrate social media conversations and "what's trending" segments. While old and new media continue to become more integrated, the line is also blurring between types of online media. *Owned media* (e.g., company website, blog), *earned media* (e.g., shares, reviews, reposts), and *paid media* (e.g., sponsored posts, ads) are becoming fused. For example, finance website The Penny Hoarder (owned media) pays guest bloggers (paid media). The Dallas Mavericks basketball team embeds its social media feed into its website (owned media) and utilizes hashtags #MFFL (Mavericks Fan For Life) to prompt others to post (earned media). Bath and bedding brand, Parachute, promotes the hashtag #MyParachuteHome for consumer content that includes the company's products. They then use the social-shared, user-generated content (earned) to develop online ads and direct mail pieces (paid media) (Greenbaum 2020). In addition, Parachute has curated social media posts under the #myparachutehome heading within product landing pages. Consumers can click on a social media post to "shop the looks you love." Other approaches that creatively blend earned and owned media are branded Snapchat lenses, Facebook filters, and TikTok branded effects. The OTC cold and flu medicine, Mucinex, created a contest asking TikTok users to dance like a zombie using the hashtag #BeatTheZombieFunk (apparently, we feel like Zombies when we have the cold and flu). Users could also use a branded effect on their videos—a dancing cartoon mascot, Mr. Mucus, superimposed over their video. This synergy of different media types paid off: over half a million videos were uploaded, the campaign had 5.8 billion views, and there was a 60.5 percentage lift in ad recall (TikTok 2022a). So, why are marketers exerting this level of interest in both shaping and spreading sWOM? You know the answer—many consumers are more likely to purchase a product after seeing it shared on social media via a friend or family member (Patton 2016). WOM marketing matters. So let's explore it together.

Traditional WOM and Electronic WOM (eWOM)

Without question, WOM marketing is powerful and perhaps one of the most persuasive factors in the consumer decision-making process. The focus on WOM marketing has grown exponentially, and with it, related marketing constructs intended to increase its potency: influencers, referral programs, brand ambassadors, viral marketing, seeding campaigns, and brand communities (Kimmel and Kitchen 2014). A growing number of companies have been created to capitalize on the power and potential of WOM. But what exactly is it, and how does word of mouth extend to the Internet?

WOM marketing is not new—but instead, our appreciation, evolving technology, and the growing number of firms and resources devoted to the topic has changed. The WOMMA trade association defines WOM marketing as "any business action that earns a customer recommendation." Academically, numerous definitions have been put forward that are typically more complicated than industry's (see Kimmel and Kitchen 2013 for a review). For example, "word of mouth is the interpersonal communication between two or more individuals, such as members of a reference group or a customer and a salesperson" (Kim, Han, and Lee 2011, 276). Or "in a post-purchase context, consumer word-of-mouth transmissions consist of informal communications directed at other consumers about the ownership, usage or characteristics of particular goods and services and/or their sellers" (Westbrook 1987, 261). Both definitions focus on the activity or the result of the activity (Kimmel and Kitchen 2013). As some of these definitions indicate, WOM communication can be either instigated by consumers *organically*, or when marketers are involved, the messages become *amplified*. Organic WOM refers to when consumers, without being prompted by marketers, discuss their product experiences. Whereas amplified WOM refers to marketing efforts to encourage consumers to amplify the WOM. This can include reaching out to influentials to spread the word and carefully crafting messages so that consumers want to share them and that are easy to be shared, creating buzz, and using referral programs. Later in this chapter, we will argue that we need to give more attention to the third type of WOM communication—*collaborative*. Collaborative can be thought of as a combination of both organic and amplified—a message that is jointly created and shared by marketers and consumers who have an interest in a product.

On the surface, WOM appears to be simple. It involves the communicator, message, and receiver. However, the WOM process is impacted by a host of contributing factors. What are the attributes of the communicator—in particular, credibility? What motivates the communicator and receiver in creating or looking for the message? How much knowledge does the receiver have about the product? How important is the product to them? How strong is the connection between the communicator and the receiver? What is the message valence—positive, negative, or neutral? What is the mode and delivery of communication?

As you can see, it gets complicated. One of the more recent complexities is understanding whether or not what we know about traditional offline WOM translates to the Internet (eWOM)—is it "old wine in new bottles"? (Hint: it's not).

*e*WOM

Over a decade ago, scholars sought to differentiate eWOM from traditional WOM, defining it as "any positive or negative statements made by potential, actual, or former customers about a product or company, which is made available to a multitude of people and institutions via the Internet" (Hennig-Thurau et al. 2004, 39). Unlike traditional WOM, which is communicated verbally, eWOM is transmitted through a variety of electronic communication channels: discussion boards, corporate websites, blogs, e-mails, chat rooms or instant messaging, social media, review websites, and newsgroups. There are numerous differences, outside of modality, between WOM and eWOM (Cheung and Thadani 2012; Chu and Kim 2011):

- **The messenger/source:** In traditional WOM, the receiver of the message is acquainted with the individual communicating it—the messenger or source. Even if the individual is somewhat of a stranger, there is a context and cues that will help discern the messenger's credibility. In eWOM, the consumer may not be aquainted with the individual. This complicates the credibility of the message and the authenticity of the messenger.
- **Many messengers and many receivers:** In "real life," WOM occurs as a one-on-one conversation between friends or in a

small gathering, whereas eWOM can be akin to one individual (or many) screaming into a packed stadium full of people that is continually turning over with new spectators.

- **Message/opinion transmitter:** In traditional WOM, there is the opinion giver and receiver. However, eWOM provides a new role—that of the message or opinion transmitter. The transmitter may be the opinion giver, receiver, or someone new. As opposed to traditional WOM where distortion is likely to occur when and if the message is shared (think "game of telephone"), in eWOM, the message can be transmitted with a higher degree of accuracy.
- **Limited privacy:** WOM conversations occur in person typically between two individuals or in a small group. In contrast, eWOM messages can be shared immediately, repeatedly, and with 100 percent accuracy to the Internet world. Messages can be accessible to the masses.
- **Asynchronous (not in real-time) communication:** WOM communications are typically synchronous. eWOM is primarily asynchronous—conversation occurs over a period that, in some cases, can span years.
- **Messages are enduring:** Unlike face-to-face conversations, which quickly fade from our memories, online communication endures, sticking around long after that initial exchange.
- **Measurable/observable:** The Internet allows us to track, observe, and measure online conversations through various online analytic tools and measures (i.e., Constant Contact, Hootsuite). This simply is not possible (to this degree) in traditional WOM (yet).
- **The speed of communication diffusion:** eWOM can spread at an exponential speed. The conversation is not limited to water cooler banter but can spread across the globe in seconds. This is particularly true within social media.
- **More communication with weak ties:** Within an online environment, there is more exposure to what is known as "weak ties." The term "weak ties" refers to "contacts with people where your relationship is based on superficial experiences

or very few connections" (Tuten and Solomon 2015, 92). For example, a casual acquaintance or a friend of a friend. In traditional WOM communication, we frequently receive messages from friends and family ("strong ties"). While communication with "strong ties" certainly occurs online, there is more exposure and interaction with "weak ties"—strangers and online-only acquaintances. At least one study found that online weak ties were more persuasive than strong ties when selecting college courses and professors (Steffes and Burgee 2009).

sWOM Defined and Explained

When the Internet was first launched, electronic content was created by a few but consumed by the masses. Consumers could only read content; they could not create it (the Web 1.0 era). At the turn of the millennium, there was a gradual shift to create a Web where Internet users were not only consumers but also creators of Web content. The Web became a place where consumers could create, engage, and collaborate with each other (the Web 2.0 era). At first, electronic communication modalities consisted primarily of online discussion forums (e.g., Yahoo! Groups), boycott websites (e.g., walmartsucks.org), and the most popular of all, opinion websites (e.g., epinions.com) (Hennig-Thurau et al. 2004). Now it includes a vast array of social platforms with varying degrees of media richness. But is WOM communication delivered via Facebook the same as those posted to a chat room or message sent via e-mail? Similarly, to the delineation of eWOM from traditional WOM, we believe that WOM communication via social media (sWOM) also deserves a more nuanced look. Specifically, we view social word of mouth (sWOM) as a subset of eWOM. We are not the first to propose reexamining and segmenting eWOM. Researchers Wang and Rodgers (2010) recognized the limitations of the earlier eWOM definition. They point out that conversations are not just positive or negative—many include mixed reviews and neutral information (Wang and Rodgers 2010). They also acknowledge the relationship between user-generated content (UGC) or consumer-generated content (CGC) (i.e., Internet content created and posted online by consumers) and eWOM, viewing eWOM as a type of UGC. Wang and Rodgers (2010) suggest that eWOM should be broken down further into two categories: informational-orientated contexts (i.e., online feedback systems and consumer review websites) and emotionally-oriented contexts (i.e., discussion boards and social networking sites). Both these typologies do not encompass all forms of electronic communication (i.e., e-mail and chat rooms or instant messaging).

In many respects, it almost sounds silly and redundant to call it sWOM. Yes, the essence of WOM is about being social. However, we argue that there is a distinct difference between WOM communication via social media and other eWOM tools, such as Instant Communication (IM) chat rooms, e-mail communication, review websites, and newsgroups.

- **Personal accounts:** In the case of eWOM, a large majority of information is shared on a company or third-party accounts. For example, a consumer writing a product review on Amazon, a concerned citizen posting a comment on a news website, or complaining about a malfunctioning product in a customer service forum. In contrast, a large percentage of sWOM is posted to and shared from a consumer's personal account. The recipients of sWOM are more likely to be connected to the poster (strong or weak ties) than are the readers of posts that appear on the company or a third-party account. This fact alone may increase the credibility and persuasiveness of the message.
- **Audience:** When a consumer posts a comment to his or her personal social media account, it has the potential to be seen by a wider assortment of consumers. In contrast, eWOMs reach may be limited to those consumers who are interested in the topic or product being discussed. For example, product reviews on Amazon are seen only by those consumers viewing the product, whereas a larger audience may see a product review posted on Facebook. Granted a consumer's Facebook friends may not have an interest in the product mentioned. However, the fact that they are exposed to the posting may have some level of influence at a later point in time.

- **Defined messenger:** Within social media, a user's communication is connected to their profile. Profile information typically consists of an image and multiple descriptors. A descriptor can be as short as a sentence (e.g., Twitter) or as long as a resume (e.g., LinkedIn). E-mail, newsgroups, review websites, and chat rooms will typically only provide a username and user address. User descriptors are an important step in building credibility and trustworthiness in WOM communications.
- **Communication direction:** Social media platforms allow for one-to-one, one-to-many, and many-to-many forms of communication between the message communicator and receiver(s) (Figure 1.2). In other words, conversations can be between individuals (e.g., private direct messages on Twitter), one-to-many (e.g., tweet to a network), but also many-to-many, where a message is created and discussed within a network (e.g., tweet using a hashtag). sWOM encompasses three communication directions, whereas traditional WOM and eWOM are limited to one or two directions.
- **Highly accessible and searchable:** Unless a user has established privacy settings, social media posts can quickly be found through searches on social media platforms, major search engines, and specialized social media monitoring tools (e.g., Hootsuite, Meltwater). In contrast, chat rooms or IM

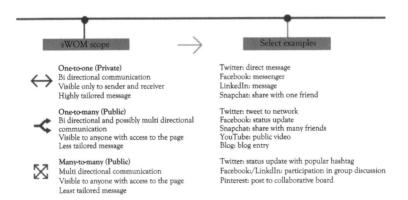

Figure 1.2 Scope of sWOM

and e-mail are not publicly searchable. It should also be noted that an increasing number of social media platforms are becoming synchronous and transient through the use of video and expiring content (i.e., Snapchat and Facebook Live).

- **Faster scalability:** Chat rooms or IM, e-mails, and newsgroups do not have the potential reach of various social media venues such as Twitter and Facebook. While an e-mail certainly has the potential to be sent far and wide, its dissemination does not match the speed and out-of-network connections that social media can. You also do not see entire TV shows and regular news segments devoted to trending e-mail.

- **Saturated information overload:** Many social media platforms (e.g., Facebook and Twitter) provide users with abundant information each time they log in. On social media, marketers face fierce competition for consumers' attention (Daugherty and Hoffman 2014). To further complicate this issue, the active lifespan of a social media post can be very short, as it becomes buried in the sea of newly created content. On a website, a product review can live forever, but on social media, the life of a message can be fleeting. The median lifespan of a tweet is a matter of minutes, and a Facebook post will get the vast majority of its impressions in the first few hours after posting (Ayres 2016).

- **Communication occurs in a mediated environment**: Communication within social media occurs primarily through their social media platform. While many platforms (e.g., Facebook and Twitter) allow for direct communications via an internal mail system, the content that is shown or is more prominently displayed is readily controlled by the platform's algorithm. Popular user posts and trending news and information, which can be commented upon, are not entirely under consumers' control.

- **More visual:** Social media is becoming an increasingly visual medium. Facebook's (now Meta's) acquisition of Instagram, the ease with which you can incorporate images and video into a tweet, and the popularity of Pinterest, Instagram, Snapchat, and TikTok all speak to consumers' ability and desire to incorporate imagery into their communication. Older forms of electronic communication, such as e-mail, are not as visually oriented.

- **Cocreation:** Social media content is frequently cocreated between consumers and between marketers and consumers (and vice versa). This is often referred to as collaborative content. Marketers can inspire conversations or the creation and sharing of images through various initiatives such as contests and hashtag campaigns. Sometimes, these conversations generate a positive result, other times, consumers can, intentionally or unintentionally, take them in a negative direction. There are many examples of where hashtags have become "bashtags." In 2014, the hashtag #myNYPD sought to encourage positive images of police officers and instead received, over one day, almost 102,000 tweets addressing various civil rights violations (Swann 2014). In some cases, marketers have also taken over existing consumer hashtags with negative consequences. In one example, Digiorno Pizza used the hashtag #WhyIStayed and included the answer—"I had Pizza." Unfortunately, the hashtag was already associated with domestic violence (cringe!). Needless to say, they quickly deleted the message and profusely apologized but not before it received wide media attention (Griner 2014). More recently, companies have tried to capitalize on hashtag political movements by lending their support via social media. L'Oreal Paris, in the wake of George Floyd's death, created an Instagram post with the message "Solidarity is worth it" along with a text description that included #BlackLivesMatter. The post was seen as disingenuous as L'Oreal Paris had previously fired the black model Munroe Bergdorf for speaking out about racial injustices. A social media backlash occurred, and L'Oreal ended up hiring Ms. Bergdorf as a Diversity and Inclusion consultant (Nesvig and Delgado 2020). There are, however, examples of positive consequences—DDB New

York used the established #FirstWorldProblems meme for their highly successful WATERisLife viral video ad campaign. The campaign featured impoverished Haitians reading various "problems" (i.e., "I hate it when my house is so big, I need two wireless routers") (Payne and Friedman 2012).

> sWOM communication is any visual or textual post about a company or their product offering that is either created independently by a consumer, created by a company, or created by a consumer in collaboration with a company and publically shared on a personal or company social media account.

We define sWOM communication as any visual or textual post about a company or their product offering that is either created independently by a consumer, created by a company, or created by a consumer in collaboration with a company and publicly shared on a personal or company social media account. This definition is broader than other WOM or eWOM definitions; in that it considers not just opinions regarding the traditional products that a company sells but also the *content* that the company disseminates via social media. The stories that brands tell via social media are part of the product and contribute to its brand equity. This idea is similar to what consulting company McKinsey has called a "consequential" type of WOM marketing, "which occurs when consumers directly exposed to traditional marketing campaigns pass on messages about them or brands they publicize" (Bughin, Doogan, and Vetvik 2010). Social media has provided countless ways to distribute a wide variety of information that consumers deem valuable enough to share. Whether a social media post includes an e-book, white paper, product photography, how-to video, recipe, or even a joke, the act of sharing itself is an endorsement or recommendation. And, while a consumer may not be directly discussing the traditional product offerings of a company, they are still disseminating and conversing about a company's offering in the form of their digital assets. This act of sharing in the social media space can be as simple as forwarding information (i.e., retweet or share), personalizing information that is created by someone else, writing product- or brand-related comments, or creating product- or brand-related content and posting it (i.e., video, photograph, etc.). The other aspect of this definition we need to highlight and explore is the intersection between consumers and companies in the social media environment (Figure 1.3). Increasingly, consumers and companies are cocreating content in both planned and organic ways.

As illustrated in Figure 1.3, sWOM communications can include one-to-one (e.g., direct message on Twitter), one-to-many (e.g., Facebook status update), or many-to-many (e.g., the use of a popular hashtag) messages. Communication can originate from a consumer, a company, or both parties can collaborate (the 3 Cs). Consumer content is created by a consumer without any involvement from a company—organic content. Examples include sharing an experience on Facebook, creating a video for YouTube, or Instagramming a photo of a recent purchase. This is commonly referred to as earned media because there is no cost to the

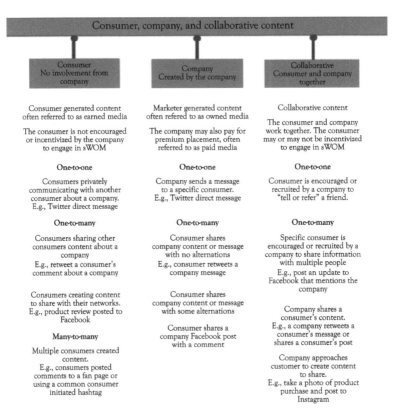

Figure 1.3 sWOM typology

company. Company-generated communication refers to the content created and posted by the company's marketing department. The company shares this communication with one or more consumers in the hope that they will engage with the content through liking, sharing, retweeting, and commenting, thereby amplifying the communication. This is commonly referred to as paid media, particularly if the company has paid to promote the communication (e.g., promoted tweet). Outside of consumer-generated and company-generated content, there is a middle ground; a combination of both organic and amplified WOM efforts—collaborative. In this instance, consumers and companies are working together to create and share information. For example, a company may invite consumers to upload photos of their purchase with a hashtag. The Parachute example offered earlier in this chapter is an example of collaborative communications. Collaborative communication has seen significant growth in recent years, thanks in part to high smartphone-adoption rates (Tode 2015). Stores are now thoughtfully integrating social media within consumers' in-store experience. Consumers are not only prompted via signage to not only "follow," "like," "Check-In," and review retail venues but also to contribute to social media conversations via a preselected and promoted hashtag.

Some stores, like Target and Victoria Secret, even craft in-store photo-ops. See Figure 1.4 for an example. Both campaigns encourage users to take photos and use their hashtags (#targetdog, #vstease, #vsgift). Victoria Secret went a step further by rewarding their consumers with a "sexy surprise" (after they showed an associate that they shared their branded selfie). Signage is also becoming more dynamic as retail is slowly starting to embrace digital signage. Perhaps, displaying consumer tweets and posts related to brands will become commonplace within stores. Companies can create contests that require consumers to create content to be shared. Another example of collaboration communications is when companies hire social influencers to tweet positive statements about the company. Depending on the strategy, collaborative communication can be a combination of earned, paid, and owned media.

Regardless of whether the sWOM is consumer- or company-generated or whether it is a collaborative effort, some forms of sWOM require more

Figure 1.4 #targetdog
Source: Courtesy of C. Munoz.

effort than others. Retweeting takes much less effort than generating a new post. Generating a new status update takes less work than creating a video and posting it on YouTube. The amount of effort required of the consumer is closely tied to consumer engagement. The topic of engagement is covered in Chapter 2, so we will not discuss it here. But for now, suffice to say that marketers need to ensure that they account for varying levels of engagement and pay more attention to consumers participating in higher level engagement forms of sWOM.

Importance of sWOM

The importance of sWOM for marketers can be summarized in two key facts. First, almost everyone online uses a social network (Mander 2016). While usage rates may vary dramatically between consumer segments, social media is touching and impacting the lives of most consumers. Second, sWOM influences each stage in the consumer decision-making process and can impact sales. Like WOM and eWOM, sWOM serves as an important information source in the prepurchase research process. The Global Web Index Survey found that social media is used by 28 percent of Internet users to find "inspiration for things" and 27 percent find products to purchase. Social media was more popular in product-related searches for younger consumers (GWI 2021, 2022). Simply put, consumers are increasingly turning to social networks and consumer reviews to hear their friends' (and strangers') opinions on products, view pictures depicting how the product "really" looks, and find new uses and applications through videos. However, the extent to which they rely on social media in their investigations depends heavily on the type of product they are considering purchasing (Bughin 2015). Outside of facilitating product research, sWOM is leading to sales. In fact, there is evidence that the COVID-19 pandemic has not only increased purchasing online but also that sWOM has been increasingly influential. A survey by Stackla found that 72 percent of consumer surveyed are spending more time online and 56 percent are more influenced by social media content since the start of the pandemic. Moreover, 79 percent indicated that user-generated social media content impacted their purchasing decisions, and 66 percent were "inspired" by other consumers' social media images to purchase a new brand (Stackla 2021). Given the increasing rates of online shopping and the growing number of technologies that integrate shopping options directly into social media posts, it is not unreasonable to expect that sWOM's direct sales influence will continue to increase.

Outside of being instrumental in product research and influencing sales, sWOM communication has other benefits. Let's look at some examples of how sWOM communication has made a difference:

- **Generate awareness or buzz:** Hershey's Cookies "N" Crème created a TikTok Gen Z-focused campaign running In-Feed Ads drawn from four popular creator accounts. The four creators also posted short videos from their personal TikTok accounts. Ultimately, TikTok videos were successful in creating brand awareness (13 million video views and a 32.8 percent lift in ad recall) (TikTok 2022b).
- **Increase social media engagement:** Popular WOM content via social media can quickly increase a brand's engagement, likes, or the number of followers on social media. Cadbury decided to honor (and elicit engagement) from their nearly one million fans of their UK Facebook page by creating a giant Facebook "like" thumb out of Cadbury milk chocolate. The result was over 40,000 new Facebook likes (in two days) and an increase of 35 percent for active fans (Bazu 2013).
- **Inspire new product ideas and resurrect old ones:** There is truth to TED Talk's slogan—"Ideas Worth Spreading." Good ideas catch on, and smart marketers look to popular sWOM messages for product inspiration. Popular organically created hashtags such as #BringBackCrystalPepsi helped inspire Pepsi to re-release this 1990s clear soda in 2016 (Mitchell 2015; PepsiCo 2016). Whereas other companies ask consumers directly to come up with new product ideas. Take, for instance, Lay's "Do Us a Flavor" contest, which asked consumers to come up with new potato chip flavors and encouraged fans to vote via social media. The flavor winner received $1 million, and consumers' taste buds were treated to exotic flavors such as Crispy Taco (2017), Southern Biscuits and Gravy (2015), Wasabi Ginger (2014), and Cheesy Garlic Bread (2013) (PepsiCo 2017).

- **Increase consumer satisfaction:** It goes without saying that you need to monitor social media conversations about your brand. Companies such as Nike and JetBlue go a step further by having dedicated Twitter handles to address consumer comments and questions. This has allowed them to provide, especially in the case of JetBlue, real-time support and frankly, happiness. Take, for instance, the story of a JetBlue customer who tweeted that he would board his 100th flight with them that year. Without knowing his name or flight (but looking up his handle and then tracking him down), they met him at his arrival gate with a banner and cupcakes (Kolowich 2014). Heck, we would have been satisfied with a retweet!
- **Raise awareness and money for nonprofit causes:** A growing number of nonprofits have been using sWOM to increase awareness for their cause and inspire donations. Facebook (now Meta) created its first platform fundraising tool in 2016. As of March 2021, Facebook and Instagram fundraising tools have raised over $5 billion in donations to nonprofits and some personal causes (Meta 2021). Many of these fundraisers are birthday fundraisers. Notable nonprofit fundraisers include the ALS association raising over $5 million St. Jude Children's Research Hospital was gifted over $100 million, and No Kid Hungry has been able to help feed kids 100 million more meals (Gleit 2019).

Our Journey Ahead

This book is not an introductory "how-to" book on social media. It is assuming that you have already gotten your feet wet (or drenched) in the topic. Instead, the purpose of this book is to examine the influence of sWOM and provide guidance on how to operationalize its growing power. Our goal in writing this book is to bring together industry best practices and academic research to illustrate how much sWOM matters. It should also help you construct social media posts that will be both shared and conform to regulatory guidelines. Each chapter highlights a key area of sWOM that will further your understanding of the topic and provide actionable information to increase the likelihood of creating your own sharable sWOM marketing successes:

The Social Consumer

The social consumer examines individuals who use social media to inform their product decisions and also share product-related information and opinions with others. This chapter explores who they are, the different roles they play, and their motivations to share. It concludes what an acknowledgment that consumers are rethinking how they should integrate social media in their lives.

The Social Business

In most companies, social media usage begins in the marketing department, but it should not end there. Social media can add value in other ways including, offering strategic insights, identifying problems, crowdsourcing ideas for new products and services, improving customer service, recruiting new employees, and empowering employees to spread positive sWOM. In this chapter, we discuss the importance of becoming a social business. We review the stages of social business development and how social tools can be integrated to become part of your company's DNA.

Storytelling

Social media posts need to tell a story and marketers need to learn to be good storytellers. This chapter explores how to construct shareable stories concentrating on not only textual content but also the importance of visual communication in all your marketing efforts.

Social Influencers and Employee Advocates

Influencer marketing has seen tremendous growth in recent years. Influencers are no longer just celebrities. In fact, companies can see more return on their investment by utilizing "everyday consumers" or even their employees. This chapter provides an overview of the different influencer types, how to select an influencer that is right for a brand, and how to implement an influencer campaign. Particular attention is also given on creating and operationalizing an employee influencer advocate program.

The Power of Persuasion

To be successful in social media and to encourage sWOM, your company needs to be influential. In this chapter, we explore six principles of persuasion as they apply to social media.

Legal and Regulatory Issues

There is a very fine line between encouraging and incentivizing consumers and employees to engage in sWOM about your brand—a line that *may* have legal implications for your company. In this chapter, we examine "material connections"—relationships that exist between a company and an endorser of your brand—and the guidelines that must be followed to ensure that consumers are not being deceived by information they learn and recommendations they receive on social media. This chapter also explores the importance of having a well-developed social media policy, the process of creating a policy and appropriate content.

References

ANA. 2020. "The State of Influence: Challenges and Opportunities in Influencer Marketing." Retrieved from www.ana.net/miccontent/show/id/rr-2020-state-of-influence.

Arthur, R. December 2, 2020. "Coca-Cola Dedicates Share a Coke to 'everyday hereos'." *Beverage Daily*. Retrieved from www.beveragedaily.com/Article/2020/12/02/Coca-Cola-marks-pandemic-year-by-dedicating-Share-a-Coke-to-everyday-heroes.

Austin, S. November 3, 2020. "Why Trust and Incentives Help Consumers With Better Brand Selection." *Entrepreneur*. Retrieved from www.entrepreneur.com/article/357871.

Ayres, S. 2016. "Shocking New Data About the Lifespan of Your Facebook Posts." Post Planner. Retrieved from www.postplanner.com/lifespan-of-facebook-posts/ (accessed June 22, 2016).

Bazu, A. 2013. "Cadbury's 'Thanks a Million' Campaign: The Sweet Taste of Success!" *UCD Graduate Business School Blog*. http://ucdblogs.ucd.ie/digitalmarketingstrategy/cadburys-thanks-million-campaign-sweet-taste-success/ (accessed February 08, 2017).

Belicove, M. November 2011. "Measuring Offline Vs. Online Word-of-Mouth Marketing." *Entrepreneur*. Retrieved from www.entrepreneur.com/article/220776.

Berger, J. 2013. *Contagious*. New York, NY: Simon and Schuster.

Bughin, J. 2015. "Getting a Sharper Picture of Social Media's Influence." *McKinsey Quarterly*. Retrieved from www.mckinsey.com/business-functions/marketing-and-sales/our-insights/getting-a-sharper-picture-of-social-medias-influence.

Bughin, J., J. Doogan, and O. Vetvik. 2010. "A New Way to Measure Word-of- Mouth Marketing." *McKinsey Quarterly*. Retrieved from www.mckinsey.com/capabilities/growth-marketing-and-sales/our-insights/a-new-way-to-measure-word-of-mouth-marketing.

Cheung, C.M.K. and D.R. Thadani. 2012. "The Impact of Electronic Word-of-Mouth Communication: A Literature Analysis and Integrative Model." *Decision Support Systems* 54, no. 1, pp. 461–470. doi: 10.1016/j.dss.2012.06.008.

Chu, S.C. and Y. Kim. 2011. "Determinants of Consumer Engagement in Electronic Word-of-Mouth (eWOM) in Social Networking Sites." *International Journal of Advertising* 30, no. 1, pp. 47–75.

Coca-Cola. 2022. "Custom Bottles Page." Coca-Cola. Retrieved from https://us.coca-cola.com/store/custom-bottles.

Daugherty, T. and E. Hoffman. 2014. "eWOM and the Importance of Capturing Consumer Attention Within Social Media." *Journal of Marketing Communications* 20, no. 1–2, pp. 82–102. doi:10.1080/13527266.2013.797764.

Deye, J. 2015. "#ShareACoke and the Personalized Brand Experience." *Marketing Insights*. Retrieved from www.ama.org/publications/eNewsletters/MarketinglnsightsNewsletter/Pages/sharecoke-and-the-personalized-brand-experience.aspx (accessed February 08, 2017).

Domo. 2020. "Data Never Sleeps 9.0." Domo. Retrieved from www.domo.com/learn/infographic/data-never-sleeps-9.

Gleit, N. 2019. "People Raise Over $2 Billion for Causes on Facebook." *Meta for Business*. Retrieved from https://about.fb.com/news/2019/09/2-billion-for-causes/.

Google; KellerFay Group. 2016. "Word of Mouth (WOM)." Retrieved from https://ssl.gstatic.com/think/docs/word-of-mouth-and-the-internet_infographics.pdf (accessed May 28, 2016).

Greenbaum, T. 2020. "7 User-Generated Content Examples and Why They Work So Well." Retrieved from https://www.bazaarvoice.com/blog/7-ugc-examples/.

Griner, D. 2014. "DiGiorno Is Really, Really Sorry About Its Tweet Accidentally Making Light of Domestic Violence." *AdWeek*. Retrieved from www.adweek.com/adfreak/digiorno-really-really-sorry-about-its-tweet-accidentally-making-light-domestic-violence-159998.

GWI. 2021. "Social Media Marketing in 2021." *Global WebIndex*. Retrieved from www.gwi.com/reports/social-report-b.

GWI. 2022. "Social Media Use By Generation." *Global WebIndex*. Retrieved from www.gwi.com/reports/social-media-across-generations.

Hennig-Thurau, T., K.P. Gwinner, G. Walsh, and D.D. Gremler. 2004. "Electronic Word-of-Mouth Via Consumer-Opinion Platforms: What Motivates Consumers to Articulate Themselves on the Internet?" *Journal of Interactive Marketing* 18, no. 1, pp. 38–52. John Wiley & Sons. doi:10.1002/dir.10073.

Hitz, L. 2014. "Simply Summer Social Awards Contestant #3 | Simply Measured." *The Simply Measured Blog*. http://simplymeasured.com/blog/simply-summer-social-awards-contestant-3-cocacolas-shareacoke-campaign/#sm.00018n9uis1172fifrc4xqq28xm0f (accessed February 08, 2017).

Kim, W.G., J.S. Han, and E. Lee. 2011. "Effects of Relationship Marketing on Repeat Purchase and Word of Mouth." *Journal of Hospitality & Tourism Research* 25, no. 3, pp. 272–288. doi:10.1177/109634800102500303.

Kimmel, A.J. and P.J. Kitchen. 2013. "WOM and Social Media: Presaging Future Directions for Research and Practice." *Journal of Marketing Communications* 20, no. 1–2, pp. 1–16. doi:10.1080/13527266.2013.797730.

Kimmel, A.J. and P.J. Kitchen. 2014. "Introduction: Word of Mouth and Social Media." *Journal of Marketing Communications* 20, no. 1–2, p. 24. Retrieved from http://ovidsp.ovid.com/ovidweb.cgi?T=JS&PAGE=reference&D=psyc11&NEWS=N&AN=2013-45151-002.

Kolowich, L. 2014. "Delighting People in 140 Characters: An Inside Look at JetBlue's Customer Service Success." *Hubspot Blog*. Retrieved from http://blog.hubspot.com/marketing/jetblue-customer-service-twitter#sm.00018n9uis1172fifrc4xqq28xm0f.

Mander, J. 2016. "97% Visiting Social Networks." *GlobalWebIndex*. www.globalwebindex.net/blog/97-visiting-social-networks.

Meta. 2021. "Coming Together to Raise $5 Billion on Facebook and Instagram." *Meta for Business*. Retrieved from www.facebook.com/business/news/coming-together-to-raise-5-billion-on-facebook-and-instagram.

Mitchell, E. 2015. "Pepsi Makes the Most of Viral #BringBackCrystal Pepsi Campaign." *Adweek*. Retrieved from www.adweek.com/performance-marketing/pepsi-makes-the-most-of-viral-bringbackcrystalpepsi-campaign/.

Nesvig, K. and S. Delgado. June 09, 2020. "Munroe Bergdorf Joins L'Oreal Paris as Consultant After Calling Out the Brand." *TeenVogue*. Retrieved from www.teenvogue.com/story/munroe-bergdorf-loreal-paris-black-lives-matter.

Nielsen. 2012. "Newswire | Consumer Trust in Online, Social and Mobile Advertising Grows." *Nielsen*. www.nielsen.com/insights/2012/consumer-trust-in-online-social-and-mobile-advertising-grows/#:~:text=According%20to%20Nielsen's%20latest%20Global,an%20increase%20of%2018%20percent.

Patton, T. 2016. "8 Statistics That Will Change the Way You Think About Referral Marketing." *Ambassador Blog*.

Payne, E. and C. Friedman. 2012. "Viral Ad Campaign Hits #FirstWorld Problems." CNN. Retrieved from www.cnn.com/2012/10/23/tech/ad-campaign-twist/.

PepsiCo. 2016. "Celebrate the 90s With Crystal Pepsi—Iconic Clear Cola to Hit Shelves This Summer." *PepsiCo Press Release*. www.pepsico.com/live/pressrelease/celebrate-the-90s-with-crystal-pepsi-iconic-clear-cola-to-hit-shelves-this-su06292016.

PepsiCo. 2017. "America Has Voted! Lay's Crispy Taco Crowned 2017 Lay's Do Us a Flavor." *Pepsico*. Retrieved from www.pepsico.com/news/press-release/america-has-voted-lays-crispy-taco-crowned-2017-lays-do-us-a-flavor-winner10112017 (accessed February 08, 2017).

Perrin, A. and S. Atske. 2021. "About Three-in-Ten U.S. Adults Say They Are 'Almost Constantly' Online." *Pew Research Center*. Retrieved from www.pewresearch.org/fact-tank/2021/03/26/about-three-in-ten-u-s-adults-say-they-are-almost-constantly-online/.

Pew Research Center. 2021. "Mobile Fact Sheet." Pew Research Center. Retrieved from www.pewresearch.org/internet/fact-sheet/mobile/.

Power Reviews. 2021. "New Consumer Survey of More Than 6,500 Consumer Reveals Increasing Importance of Product Reviews to Establish Trust and Drive Purchase Behavior." *GlobeNewswire*. Retrieved from www.globenewswire.com/news-release/2021/05/20/2233533/0/en/New-Consumer-Survey-of-More-than-6-500-Consumers-Reveals-Increasing-Importance-of-Product-Reviews-to-Establish-Trust-and-Drive-Purchase-Behavior.html.

Smith, A. 2011. "Smartphone Adoption and Usage." Retrieved from www.pewinternet.org/2011/07/11/smartphone-adoption-and-usage/.

Stackla. 2021. "Post-Pandemic Shifts in Consumer Shopping Habits: Authenticity, Personalization and the Power of UGC." *Stackla*. Retrieved from https://stackla.com/resources/reports/post-pandemic-shifts-in-consumer-shopping-habits-authenticity-personalization-and-the-power-of-ugc/.

Steffes, E.M. and L.E. Burgee. 2009. "Social Ties and Online Word of Mouth." *Internet Research* 19, no. 1, pp. 42–59.

Swann, P. 2014. "NYPD Blues: When a Hashtag Becomes a Bashtag." *Public Relations Society of America*. www.prsa.org/Intelligence/TheStrategist/Articles/view/10711/1096/NYPD_Blues_When_a_Hashtag_Becomes_a_Bashtag#.V3PeIvkrKM8 (accessed February 08, 2017).

Tadena, N. July 15, 2014. "Coke's Personalized Marketing Campaign Gains Online Buzz—CMO Today—WSJ." *The Wall Street Journal*. Retrieved from http://blogs.wsj.com/cmo/2014/07/15/cokes-personalized-marketing-campaign-gains-online-buzz/.

Thomson, T.J., D. Angus, and P. Dootson. 2020. "3.2 Billion Images and 720,000 Hours of Video Are Shared Online Daily. Can You Sort Real From Fake?" *The Conversation*. Retrieved from https://theconversation.com/3-2-billion-images-and-720-000-hours-of-video-are-shared-online-daily-can-you-sort-real-from-fake-148630.

TikTok. 2022a. "Mucinex." *TikTok for Business*. Retrieved from www.tiktok.com/business/en/inspiration/mucinex-98.

TikTok. 2022b. "Hershey's Cookies 'n' Crème." *TikTok for Business*. Retrieved from https://us.tiktok.com/business/en-US/inspiration/hershey's-cookies-'n'-cr%C3%A8me-365.

Tode, C. August 10, 2015. "Retailers Adapt Social Media for Real-World, In-Store Sales Impact." *Mobile Commerce Daily*. Retrieved from www.mobilecommercedaily.com/retailers-adapt-social-media-for-real-world-in-store-sales-impact.

Tuten, T. and M.R. Solomon. 2015. *Social Media Marketing*. Thousand Oaks, CA: Sage Publications.

Wang, Y. and S. Rodgers. 2010. "Electronic Word of Mouth and Consumer Generated Content: From Concept to Application." In *Handbook of Research on Digital Media and Advertising: User Generated Content Consumption*, ed. M. Eastin, pp. 212–231. New York, NY: Information Science Reference. doi:10.4018/978-1-60566-792-8.ch011.

We Are Social and Hootsuite. 2022. "Digital 2022 Global Overview Report." Retrieved from https://wearesocial.com/uk/blog/2022/01/digital-2022-another-year-of-bumper-growth-2/.

Westbrook, R.A. 1987. "Product/Consumption-Based Affective Responses and Postpurchase Processes." *Journal of Marketing Research* 24, pp. 258–271. doi:10.2307/3151636.

Whitler, K. 2014. "Why Word of Mouth Marketing Is the Most Important Social Media." *Forbes*. www.forbes.com/sites/kimberlywhitler/2014/07/17/why-word-of-mouth-marketing-is-the-most-important-social-media/#3443d9c37a77.

WOMMA. 2014. "Return on Word of Mouth." Retrieved from https://womma.org/wp-content/uploads/2015/09/STUDY-WOMMA-Return-on-WOM-Executive-Summary.pdf (accessed February 08, 2017).

CHAPTER 2

The Social Consumer

It may feel like everyone (and their grandmother) spends their entire day liking, tweeting, and creating TikTok videos—yet, that is not the reality. Everyone is not spending extensive time on social media and those who are do not use every social media platform. Over time, consumers change their social media platform preferences and behavior. Just because a consumer group is using a platform today offers no guarantee that they will be using the same platform tomorrow. Indeed, social media is a fluid and evolving space. Many of the changes that occur in social media can be attributed to technological advancements and perhaps, more importantly, consumer behavior. The future of social media platforms, such as Facebook and Instagram, and the manner in which consumers use them to both connect with companies and engage in sWOM are dependent on each platform's ability to meet consumer needs. Therefore, to be successful in your social media efforts, it is crucial to understand social media consumer behavior. So, who is the social consumer and why should we care?

What Is a Social Consumer?

A social consumer is an individual who uses social media to both identify and share product-related information (i.e., articles and opinions) that assists their own or others' consumption decision-making process. A social consumer may use Facebook to checkout a friend's new outfit, LinkedIn to establish the credibility of a local home improvement company, Twitter to keep abreast of breaking industry news, YouTube to learn how to build a bookcase from Lowes, and Pinterest to bookmark future purchases. In other words, consumers are using social media to help them identify, evaluate, and use products and services. They are both viewing and engaging in communication with their personal networks and businesses. In addition, they are sharing information and offering their opinion on products, thereby potentially influencing the behavior of others. This chapter will explore the demographic and behavioral differences behind these consumers.

Who Are Social Consumers?

> 4.62 billion individuals or over half of the world's population are active social media users.

Globally, 4.62 billion individuals are active social media users and virtually everyone is accessing their social media accounts from a mobile device (We Are Social and Hootsuite 2022). The heaviest users of social media, specifically social networking sites (SNS), are the young (e.g., 2021: 84 percent of 18–29-year-olds); however, older consumers are adopting SNS at an increasing rate. Between 2010 and 2021, usage among those aged 65 and over more than tripled (11 to 45 percent) (Auxier and Anderson 2021). Adoption rates are also tied to education and income. Consumers with a higher level of education and income are the most likely to use social media (Auxier and Anderson 2021). Historically, in the United States, it was women who boasted the highest use of social media. Today, the gender gap has somewhat narrowed. In 2021, 78 percent of women online used SNS compared to 66 percent of men (Auxier and Anderson 2021). However, gender differences do exist for specific social media platforms. To illustrate, Pinterest, Snapchat, TikTok, Instagram, and Facebook are more frequently used by women. Pinterest is used almost three times more by women than men. YouTube and Twitter have comparable adoption rates for both genders, whereas LinkedIn, WhatsApp, and Reddit are more popular with men (Auxier and Anderson 2021).

Social media platforms' adoption rates also vary by race and ethnicity. A 2021 study by Pew Research Center revealed that while Facebook is the most popular platforms across racial or ethnic lines, minority groups (i.e., Blacks and Hispanics) have considerably higher rates of platform usage, compared to Whites on most of the popular SNS (i.e., Facebook, Instagram, YouTube, WhatsApp, and TikTok). Notably, Hispanics usage rates are much higher on WhatsApp (46 percent) compared to Whites (16 percent) and Blacks (23 percent) and lower on LinkedIn (19 percent, versus Black 27 percent and White 29 percent) and Pinterest (18 versus 35 percent Black and 34 percent White).

Figure 2.1 outlines the number of active users for each platform

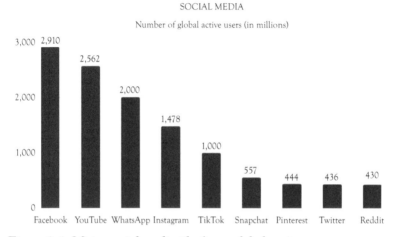

Figure 2.1 Major social media platforms global active users
Source: Data curated from We Are Social and Hootsuite (2022).

Consumers across the globe have adopted an average of 7.5 different social media platforms. In the United States, adoption rates are slightly lower, with the average consumer using 6.6 different platforms (We Are Social and Hootsuite 2022). If consumers are limiting their social media usage to just one platform, chances are it is Facebook. Facebook remains the worldwide favorite and the overall favorite in the United States (although a teen or young adult will passionately debate this point) (GWI 2022). Yet, more U.S. adults use YouTube (81 versus 69 percent for Facebook). After YouTube and Facebook, there is a steep drop-off for U.S. adult social media platform reported 2021 usage—Instagram (40 percent), Pinterest (31 percent), LinkedIn (28 percent), Snapchat (25 percent), WhatsApp (23 percent), TikTok (21 percent), Reddit (18 percent), and Nextdoor (13 percent) (Pew Research Center 2021a).

Social media platform usage, however, does not exemplify frequency of use or the demographic differences that exist. To illustrate, average daily time spent on social media can vary dramatically by county. Philippines residents are on it, on average 4 hours and 6 minutes, whereas individuals in Japan clock in at only 51 minutes a day. United States consumers fall somewhere in-between at 2 hours and 14 minutes (We Are Social and Hootsuite 2022). As for the frequency of use, a majority of U.S. adults are likely to use Facebook, Snapchat, Instagram, and YouTube on a daily basis, whereas Twitter is used daily by only 46 percent of those surveyed (Pew Research Center 2021a). In fact, 49 percent of U.S. Facebook users (Gramlich 2021) and 38 percent of Instagram users use it several times a day (Schaeffer 2021).

How and Why Do Social Consumers Access Social Media?

In 2021, smartphone adoption rates (85 percent) were higher than desktop and laptop computers (77 percent). Adoption rates for tablets were at 53 percent (Pew Research Center 2021b). Young adults have even higher adoption rates—96 percent of 18- to 29-year-olds and 95 percent of 30- to 49-year-olds own a smartphone (Pew Research Center 2021b). But, smartphones aren't just for adults; in 2018, 95 percent of U.S. teenagers had access to a smartphone (Anderson and Jiang 2018). Outside of age, smartphone ownership in the United States is somewhat equally divided between men and women but skewed toward younger, college-educated consumers earning higher incomes. Ownership rates are approximately the same between Whites, Blacks, and Hispanics (Pew Research Center 2021b). For 15 percent of smartphone consumers, their smartphone is their primary, if not only, means to access the Internet. They do not have a broadband connection (Perrin 2021). Outside of simple access, it appears that consumers are spending considerably more time using social media on their smartphones compared to their desktop or laptop computers. Worldwide, 98.8 percent of all social media users access platforms on their mobile phones (We Are Social and Hootsuite 2021).

There is a myriad of reasons why consumers access social media. A 2020 study conducted by GWI (Global WebIndex) of 180,852 worldwide Internet users aged 16 to 64 identified the most popular reasons behind social media consumption (see the following bulleted list). In addition, they completed later a generational analysis to determine if motivations differed between Gen Z (1997–2003), Millennials (1983–1996), Gen X (1964–1982), and Boomers (1955–1963). While some motivations remained relatively constant between generations (e.g., "keeping in touch," "reading news stories," and "finding products to purchase"). Other motivations such as "filling spare time," "finding content," "seeing what's trending," "finding inspiration," "following celebrities or influencers," "seeing brand updates," and "making new contacts" were vastly different especially when comparing Gen Z to Baby Boomers. In general, each of these motivating reasons was most popular for Generation Z and gradually decreased for each subsequent generation. The one exception was "keeping in touch with friends/family" where Baby Boomers had the highest affirmative response, followed subsequently by each generation (GWI 2021, 2022).

- Keeping in touch with friends/family—50 percent
- Filling spare time—37 percent
- Reading news stories—36 percent
- Finding content—32 percent
- Seeing what's trending/being talked about—30 percent
- Finding inspiration for things—28 percent
- Finding products to purchase—27 percent
- Sharing/discussing opinions with others—25 percent
- Watching livestreams—24 percent
- Making new contacts—24 percent
- Seeing updates/content from favorite brands—23 percent
- Work-related networking research—23 percent
- Finding like-minded communities—22 percent
- Posting about your life—22 percent
- Watching/following sports—21 percent
- Following celebrities or influencers—21 percent

Thankfully, from a marketer's perspective, many of these motivating reasons revolve around brands and their marketing efforts. It is clear that social media is part of the consumer buyer's journey. This is particularly true for younger generations that are more apt to follow influencers, research brands, and get brand recommendations.

Levels of Engagement and Social Consumer Roles

Social media satisfies a variety of purposes—it allows us to stay in touch with friends, network with professionals, stay current with news or events, provides entertainment, but it also provides us with the opportunity to share our opinions simultaneously with a large number of consumers and to engage with brands. Social consumers play various roles that impact the consumer decision-making process: social listeners, social sharers, and social influencers. Before we delve into these roles, let's first examine the levels of engagement possible within social media.

Charlene Li's, Senior Fellow at Altimeter, research developed an engagement pyramid (Figure 2.2). The engagement pyramid depicts various levels of engagement that social consumers and social employees can have within social media. It reveals that many consumers and employees are engaged at the lower levels. Although this research is now dated, these categories still hold in the context of social media. Smartphone ubiquity, coupled with the popularity of image and video platforms such as Instagram, Snapchat, and TikTok, suggests that we may need to rethink the placement of producing on the pyramid.

The *Watching* segment's engagement is limited to watching (or listening) to social media. In academic and industry research, these are commonly referred to as Lurkers (Gong, Lim, and Zhu 2015). They are

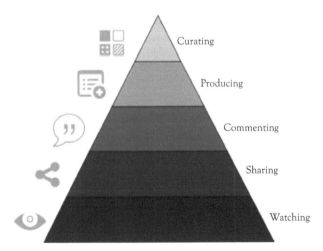

Figure 2.2 The social media engagement pyramid
Source: Adapted from Li (2010).

passive observers of tweets, Instagram posts, and articles that they see on Facebook and videos they watch on YouTube. They are neither sharing nor interacting but simply consuming information. Industry experts originally claimed that as much as 90 percent of social media were classified as Lurkers (Nielsen 2006). Others have since claimed that this number may be inflated (Vision Critical 2014; Dembosky 2012). But regardless of the actual number, all agree that the majority of consumers are simply watching. The second level is *Sharing*. At this level, consumers become more engaged—they are not only listening and digesting information, but they are also frequent sharers of information. They retweet and share content produced by other individuals and companies' content. *Commenting* is the next level, where consumers craft and share their opinions. Their opinions are not private but rather part of a larger public dialog. Arguably, the next two steps take a considerable jump up in the engagement level when compared to commenting. In *Producing,* consumers create fresh new content (e.g., YouTube videos, Facebook posts) to share with others. The last level of engagement, *Curation,* is only accomplished by a small number of consumers. These individuals are very active on social media, sorting through content and sharing only the most relevant data with their networks. They make it easy for consumers to find what is important and relevant, and for that reason, they are seen as trusted advisers (Li 2010). As a company, you don't want all of your consumers to simply watch (or listen) to your social media content. If all they do is watch, then their level of influence is low. Instead, you should strive to develop content that moves some of consumers up to higher levels of the engagement pyramid.

The three roles of social listeners, social sharers, and social influencers are related to engagement—although they are somewhat broader constructs (Figure 2.3).

Social Listeners

A social listener, as the name implies, is an individual who observes or listens to conversations on social media. They participate in the "watching" level of engagement. This individual may be in a passive or active shopping mode. A passive shopping mode is when "information and advice [that] consumer[s] need to make a purchase comes to them

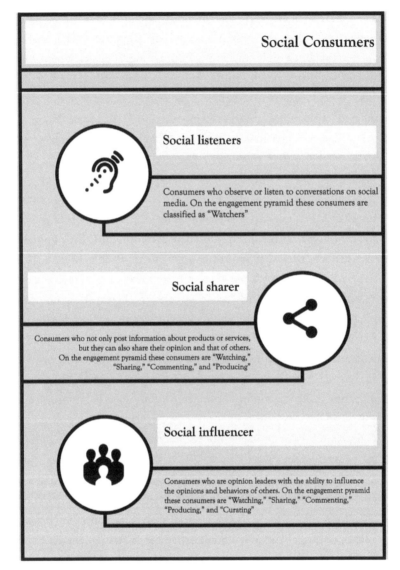

Figure 2.3 Social consumers

unsolicited" (Belch and Belch 2014, 131). Consumers are continually collecting information that may come from a Facebook post, a tweet that they happen to glance at, or a pin that they came across when looking for a great guacamole recipe. Although consumers may not be interested in purchasing the product then, the fact that they have read the post allows them to accumulate knowledge that may be helpful to them in the future or that they can share with others. For example, reading a review of a restaurant posted by a friend and then later sharing this information with another friend who is looking for a new place to eat. In truth, consumers are constantly in this passive stage—unknowingly accumulating knowledge for future use.

In the active shopping mode, consumers are "purposefully seeking information and/or assistance so [consumers] can make informed purchase decisions with confidence" (Belch and Belch 2014, 131). This hunt for product information often leads consumers to social media. A study undertaken by Forrester Research revealed that an average U.S. adult uses social media to both "discover" and "explore" new products (Fleming 2016). Whereas, a GWI 2021 study identified "finding products to purchase" as a main reason to use social media by 27 percent of North American survey respondents (GWI 2021). Younger consumers (Gen Z, Gen Y, and Gen X) are more likely to use social media to both find new products to purchase and see updates or content from their favorite brands compared to older consumers (Baby Boomers) (GWI 2022). Finding information about products and brands was also one of the three primary reasons given by consumers in using Pinterest, LinkedIn, Instagram, Reddit, and Twitter. The location of where consumers find information on new brand/product information also varies: social media ads (28 percent), recommendations/comments on social media (23 percent), updates on brands' social media pages (17 percent), posts/reviews by expert bloggers (16 percent), celebrity endorsements (15 percent), messaging app ads (14 percent), vlogs (13 percent), and forums/message boards (12 percent) (GWI 2021).

When Do They Listen?

Let's face it; we are not always receptive to other people's advice. Sometimes, we simply don't care that Sally loves her new car, found a new recipe on Pinterest, or looks fabulous in those Instagrammed shoes. But there are other times when we are not only interested but are more receptive to these social recommendations to assist us in our purchase. We are certainly more receptive when we are in active shopping mode—but are there other factors that make us more likely to listen to sWOM?

Academic research on traditional WOM and eWOM, coupled with industry studies addressing social media, has identified several conditions when social consumers are more likely to seek out and are receptive to social recommendations and information:

- Purchasing a product for the first time or having little experience within the product category (Gilly et al. 1998).
- High involvement purchase (e.g., higher level of risk associated with the purchase) (Beatty and Smith 1987).
- Younger consumers (Mixon 2016; Sprout Social 2021).
- Americans with more than $100,000 yearly household income (Mixon 2016).
- When the message is personalized and effectively targeted (Bughin 2015).
- For specific product categories (i.e., 40–50 percent of consumers used social recommendations when selecting travel and investment services) (Bughin 2015).
- Consumers who use a search engine in researching a product are also more likely to use social media in their prepurchase investigation (Bughin 2015).
- When the recommendation is received from a highly credible source (Park and Lee 2009; Gilly et al. 1998).
- Influence is more substantial when the "tie strength" is strong. In other words, your relationship or connection with the recommender is robust (i.e., friends or family) (Brown and Reingen 1987).

In conclusion, listening behavior is now swiftly converting to purchases within social media as these platforms continue to monetize. One industry survey found that approximately 8 in 10 businesses are currently selling or plan on selling directly within social media platform in the next three years (Sprout Social 2021).

Social Sharers

Not all social media users share information. Yet, many of us do share, retweet, and comment. Social sharers are consumers who not only post information about products or services via social media, but they can also share their opinion and that of others. These consumers are sharing, commenting, and producing. One industry study found that 94 percent of social media users post content on social media, 42 percent post content at least once a day, and 30 percent surveyed are either liking, posting, or sharing content more than 10 times a day (Herhold 2019). Their level of engagement on social media can include not only sharing but also commenting and even creating content.

There are two types of social sharing: implicit sharing—that relates to products (e.g., sharing a news article involving a product or endorsing a company through a "like") and explicit sharing—sharing that includes a discussion about a product (e.g., creating a post that explicitly discusses a product). Both types are influential. A 2015 Adobe Study of European social media users (UK, France, Germany, Sweden, and Netherlands) found that implicit (i.e., follows or likes) and explicit endorsements (i.e., mentions) varied by platform, with endorsements more prevalent on Facebook and Instagram compared to Snapchat. Interestingly, 18- to 24-year-olds depended considerably more on the visually oriented platform Instagram (72 percent) than the average social media user (Watt 2016).

Implicit sharing can come in many forms. It can be simply retweeting a news article without providing a personalized comment or providing a simple brand endorsement. In other words, the endorsement is implied.

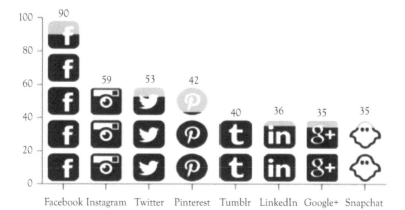

Figure 2.4 *Percentage of consumers who have made implicit and explicit endorsements on social media*

Source: Watt (2016).

A "like" on Facebook or Instagram, a "favorite" on Twitter, and a "follow" on Facebook are some of the many examples of quick implicit brand endorsements. This form of endorsement is very common perhaps, partly, to the ease at which a consumer can communicate their support. For example, a GWI survey of global social media users found that 23 percent have liked or followed a brand in the last month (GWI 2021).

Explicit brand endorsements are more involved. They can be textual, visual, or both. Textual endorsements include personalized messages, comments, or hashtags, which may be attached to an existing piece of communication. For example, retweeting an article and including a comment and a hashtag. Hashtags can be a fast and effective way of endorsing a product (e.g., #ShareaCoke, #WantAnR8, #ShareYourEars, #PepsiPerfect). Consumers can also embed their product endorsements through visual communication. For instance, a consumer may model their new Gucci sunglasses on Instagram or pin an image of a Pottery Barn couch they are planning to purchase to their personal decorating board on Pinterest. They can also do all three—post a picture with a comment and a hashtag. This type of sharing represents a higher level of engagement, requires more time and effort, and may be more influential.

Some of the most involved product discussions on social media describe a consumer's experience with a product and customer service. Both positive and negative brand experiences are commonly shared via social media. In addition, a 2020 survey by the CFI group found that approximately 18 percent of respondents shared their customer service experience on a variety of social media platforms: Facebook (39 percent), Instagram (15 percent), YouTube (15 percent), and Twitter (13 percent) (CFI Group 2020). The product discussions may contain textual descriptions of a product's strengths and weaknesses, but they may also include images and video. These visual modes of communication are powerful in their ability to influence (Chapter 6). Including hashtags can increase the likelihood of the post being discovered in a search.

Why Do We Share?

There are many reasons behind why we share within social media. Some studies have addressed this question broadly, whereas others have examined sharing behavior within specific social media platforms. Understanding what drives consumers to push the "retweet" or "share" button directly impacts the type of content and conversation you hope to have with your target market.

In 2011, the *New York Times* conducted a comprehensive U.S.-based study examining the motivations behind social media sharing. The "Psychology of Sharing" study involved ethnographies, focus groups, and a survey of 2,500 social sharers across various social media platforms. The researchers identified five separate motivations for sharing: "to bring valuable and entertaining content to others; to define ourselves to others; to grow and nourish our relationships; self-fulfillment; and to get the word out about causes or brands" (*The New York Times* 2011). Underlining each of these motives was the importance of relationships. In addition, the study identified "six personas of online sharers" (*The New York Times* 2011):

- Altruists: Individuals motivated to share information by a sense of helping others. These people are described as helpful, reliable, thoughtful, and connected.
- Careerists: For these individuals, sharing is concentrated on information related to career and reputation enhancement.
- Hipsters: Hipsters share to express their identity. They are creative, young, on the cutting-edge, and popular.
- Boomerangs: For boomerangs, sharing is linked to validation. These individuals are seeking feedback from others.
- Connectors: For these individuals, sharing is linked to making, planning, and connecting to their offline lives (e.g., sharing a deal for a brunch with friends).
- Selectives: Selectives are not frequent sharers, but they are thoughtful. They only share when the information is relevant or useful to others.

Other studies examining consumers' motivation to use social media revealed similar results. For instance, a 2016 study from Fractl of 2,000 Facebook users found that people shared third-party content primarily to entertain (48 percent), express information on issues that they valued (17 percent), evoke emotions (13 percent), and educate (11 percent).

Sixty-nine percent of respondents also indicated that sharing "helps them feel close to their friends" (Jones 2016). Both of these studies reveal somewhat similar themes—consumers are sharing information that can bring value to other people's lives. For information to be shared, it needs to be interesting, funny, or unique. We share information out of a desire to help others (e.g., altruists). We also share information to help form our identities (e.g., hipsters). Through social media, we project to others what we want to believe and want others to believe about us.

So, which persona or personas does your target market fall into? Are they hipsters? Careerists? Both? What motivates your consumers? This *New York Times* sharing typology may help guide your content planning and marketing message. However, it would be helpful for you to analyze your target market sharing behavior on your social media platforms and perform primary research exploring their specific sharing motivations.

Thus far, we have talked about general sharing motives, but what motivates us to engage with brands online and share information about our product experiences? To begin, there are several reasons why consumers "like" and follow a brand. The top reasons are to learn about products, be entertained, obtain news and promotions and connect with similar people (Nanji 2019). Academic studies addressing traditional WOM (although still applicable for sWOM) have identified several factors that increase the likelihood of sharing product experiences. Briefly, consumers often post about products when they are very satisfied or very dissatisfied (Bowman and Narayandas 2001; Anderson 1998) when the product is new (Richins and Bloch 1986; Bone 1992), when there is high product involvement (i.e., the product is relevant to consumers) (Richins and Bloch 1986), and when the consumer is highly involved in the marketplace (i.e., market mavens) (Slama and Tashcian 1985).

Marketers need to understand sharing behavior to identify the type of content that is most likely to be shared on each social media platform. Unfortunately, the act of sharing does not mean that that individual will be influential. A social consumer can post a rave review about a product, but what if that consumer has only a handful of followers and what if they never see the review? In this case, the social sharer may have limited influence on the behavior of others. For that reason, it is important the companies seek out social influencers.

Social Influencers

There are a relatively small number of social consumers that have a disproportionately large amount of social influence when it comes to sWOM. In the marketing world, they are commonly referred to as opinion leaders, social influencers, or simply, influencers. Influencers (or opinion leaders) typically focus their expertise in a specific area (i.e., fashion, food, exercise). Social influencers, those who influence the opinions and behaviors of others, are engaged at all levels—they share, comment, produce, and curate. Their recommendations are surprisingly powerful. A joint study by Twitter and Annalect found that recommendations from influencers on Twitter were relied upon almost as much as recommendations from friends (56 percent relied on friends versus 49 percent for influences). Forty percent of those surveyed admitted to purchasing a product as a result of an influencer's recommendation (Swant 2016).

Marketers recognize the importance and value of these influencers, which is why formal influencer campaigns, and the agencies that support them have become commonplace. A 2022 survey of 1000+ marketing professionals found that 34 percent were going to prioritize influencer marketing. Additionally, 57 percent of marketers currently using influencer marketing believed it was effective, and 46 percent of those planned to spend more in 2022 (Bump 2022). Influencer programs effectively fulfill three objectives: building brand awareness, generating sales leads, and increasing consumer loyalty.

Social influencers come in various forms, with varying levels of influence. They can provide companies with informal, organic support (or nonsupport). Alternatively, their role can also be much more formal, with input and compensation provided by the company. Indeed, influencer marketing has exploded—spending is estimated to be $16.4 billion in 2022 (Influencer Marketing Hub 2022). It has become an industry in itself, which includes dedicated companies, software packages, agents, and, of course, millions of influencers. To do this topic justice, we needed an entire chapter of material. So, please see Chapter 5 for an in-depth social influencers dive.

Rethinking Being a Social Consumer

Consumers are increasingly examining the role that social media is playing in their lives. This can be attributed, in part, to numerous public scandals that have embroiled social platforms. To illustrate, the 2018 Cambridge Analytica Facebook news alerted the public to the misuse of consumer data—violating the privacy of approximately 87 million Facebook users (Confessore 2018). The security of these networks has also been questioned, as evidenced by the July 15, 2020, Twitter Hack, where numerous high-profile accounts were taken over in a Bitcoin scam (New York State Department of Financial Services 2020). And most recently, in 2021, the social media platform Facebook (now Meta) has employed a host of troubling, unethical business practices. Specifically, Ms. Frances Haugen, a former Facebook product manager turned whistle blower, revealed that Meta had a two-tier content monitoring system—often letting celebrities, politicians, and other high-profile account post and disseminate content that were clear content policy violations (Horwitz 2021). Meta has also been criticized for a lack of content monitoring in developing countries where Facebook has been used to recruit women for human trafficking, run cartel businesses, and incite violence (Scheck, Purnell, and Horwitz 2021). Lastly, Instagram's (another Meta property) own internal research has found that one in five teens acknowledged that Instagram "makes them feel worse about themselves," and many teens believe that Instagram is hurting their mental health (Wells, Horwitz, and Seetharaman 2021). More broadly, 12 percent of users "report engaging in compulsive use of social media that impacts their sleep, work, parenting, or relationships."

Outside of news stories, a growing body of academic research also supports the idea that there is a correlation between heavy social media use and a variety of mental health disorders (i.e., depression, narcissism, anxiety, etc.) (Barry et al. 2017; Woods and Scott 2016; Anderson, Pallesen, and Griffiths 2017). Younger consumers (Gen Z) are the most concerned about time spent on social media (GWI 2021). Negative news stories and research coupled with consumers' own experiences of social media use have led a majority of consumers to believe that specific social media platforms, such as Facebook, have a negative impact on society (*The Washington Post* 2021). Consumers simply don't trust many of the platforms. A 2021 poll revealed that 72 percent of users did "not much" or "at all" trust Facebook, followed by TikTok 63 percent, Instagram 60 percent, WhatsApp 53 percent, and YouTube 53 percent (*The Washington Post* 2021).

Response to Public Concerns

Apple Investors, concerned with the academic literature on the negative effects of "screen time" on children, called upon Apple to find ways to reduce time spent on the iPhone (Walton 2018). What resulted was the 2018 "Screen Time" iOS tool that allows parents (and really anyone) to monitor and control how much time they spend online and notably within specific social media platforms. These monitoring features are now offered on all phone operating systems. Outside of simply monitoring social media use, some consumers have gone a step further. A Pew Research Center 2018 study found that 42 percent have "taken a break from checking in for several weeks or more" and 26 percent have deleted the Facebook phone app (Perrin 2018). While specific numbers are hard to come by, anecdotal evidence of a quitting social media trend is apparent through the plethora of "how to delete [social media platform]" articles and the popularity of the search phrases "how to delete [platform] account" for Instagram and Facebook (i.e., approximately one million combined Google keyword searches in November 2021!). The Facebook platform, however, may be experiencing the brunt of the social media exodus. Younger users are leaving. In the data presented to Congress, Facebook has seen declining use of 18- to 24-year-olds and plateauing usage of 13- to 17-year-olds since 2012 (Wagner and McLaughlin 2021). Since 2019, teenage use of Facebook has decreased by 13 percent. More troubling for Facebook is that in the next two years, it was projected to decrease by 45 percent (Heath 2021).

As everyday users are turning away from social media platforms, businesses are also responding by no longer using their accounts and no longer advertising within the network. For example, in July 2020, a coordinated Facebook advertising boycott of more than 1,000 companies, named #StopHateForProfit, occurred, whereas other companies, such as Proctor and Gamble, Walmart, and Geico, reduced their spending (Hsu and Lutz 2020). This boycott wanted Facebook to address hate speech, voter suppression, and the "silencing of Black voices" (Aziz 2020). Responding to negative news and societal pushback, some businesses have decided to make a more permanent disconnection from social media. Lush, a British cosmetics retailer with an emphasize for ethically sourced products and charity work, decided to shut down its accounts on Facebook, Instagram, Snapchat, and TikTok—losing over 10 million followers and related sales (Wood 2021). Fashion brands Bottega Veneta and Balenciaga have also eliminated their social media use (Webb 2021). Whereas others, like Patagonia, had stayed on the platform but no longer participates in the advertising business (Ali 2021).

In recent years, CEOs and senior executives from Facebook (Meta), Twitter, Google (Alphabet), Snapchat, TikTok, and Reddit have been repeatedly called into U.S. congressional hearings to address concerns regarding privacy, mental health, misinformation, political interference, and "domestic violent extremism" (C-SPAN 2020; Kang 2021; United States House 2022). Time will tell whether the state or federal government will become more involved in regulating social media. What is clear, however, is that the public is becoming more amenable to some sort of intervention. In a 2021 Washington Post–Schar School poll, 64 percent of survey respondents indicated that the "government should do more to regulate how Internet companies handle privacy issues" (*The Washington Post* 2021). Whereas Pew Research Center found that 48 percent of U.S. adults believed that the U.S. "government should take steps to restrict false information, even it if means losing some freedom …" (Mitchell and Walker 2021).

Marketing Implications

Distrust of platforms, increased privacy settings, limiting usage, deleting social media apps, and unethical business practices all have implications for marketers using social media platforms. While the authors believe that social media will not leave us anytime soon, marketers must pay attention to the changing public perceptions of specific social media platforms. In particular, they need to quickly pivot to new platforms as their target market usage patterns and platform perceptions change. Brands also need to ensure that their actions are consistent with their positioning. If a brand promotes ethical practices and consumers' well-being and health, then advertising on platforms that are antithetical to these themes would not be "on-brand." Lastly, federal regulations may be put into place limiting marketers' effectiveness in reaching their target market (see Chapter 7 for more on this topic).

References

Ali, S. October 09, 2021. "Patagonia Doubles Down on Its Facebook Boycott in Wake of New Whistleblower Leaks." *The Hill*. Retrieved from https://tinyurl.com/uvhh7bme.

Anderson, E. 1998. "Customer Satisfaction and Word of Mouth." *Journal of Service Research* 1, no. 1, pp. 5–17.

Anderson, M. and J. Jiang. May 31, 2018. "Teens, Social Media and Technology." *Pew Research Center*. Retrieved from https://www.pewresearch.org/internet/2018/05/31/teens-social-media-technology-2018/

Anderson, C., S. Pallesen, and M. Griffiths. January 2017. "The Relationship Between Addictive Use of Social Media, Narcissism, and Self-Esteem: Findings From a Large National Study." *Addictive Behaviors* 64, pp. 287–293.

Auxier, B. and M. Anderson. April 07, 2021. "Social Media Use 2021." *Pew Research Center*. Retrieved from https://www.pewresearch.org/internet/2021/04/07/social-media-use-in-2021/.

Aziz, A. June 24, 2020. "Facebook Ad Boycott Campaign 'Stop Hate for Profit' Gathers Momentum and Scale: Inside the Movement for Change." *Forbes*. Retrieved from https://www.forbes.com/sites/afdhelaziz/2020/06/24/facebook-ad-boycott-campaign-stop-hate-for-profit-gathers-momentum-and-scale-inside-the-movement-for-change/?sh=9e9004b16687.

Barry, C., C. Sidoti, S. Briggs, S. Reiter, and R. Lindsey. 2017. "Adolescent Social Media Use and Mental Health from Adolescent and Parent Perspectives." *Journal of Adolescence* 61, pp. 1–11.

Beatty, S. and S. Smith. 1987. "External Search Efforts: An Investigation Across Several Product Categories." *Journal of Consumer Research* 14, no. 1, pp. 83–95.

Belch, G. and M. Belch. 2014. "The Role of New and Traditional Media in the Rapidly Changing Marketing Communications Environment." *International Journal on Strategic Innovation Marketing* 1, no. 3, pp. 130–136.

Bone, P. 1992. "Determines of Word-of-Mouth Communications During Product Consumption." In *Advances in Consumer Research*, eds. J.F. Sherry and B. Sternthal, pp. 572–583. Provo, UT: Association for Consumer Research. www.acrwebsite.org/search/view-conference-proceedings.aspx?Id=7359.

Bowman, D. and D. Narayandas. 2001. "Managing Customer-Initiated Contacts With Manufacturers: The Impact of Share of Category Requirements and Word-of-Mouth Behavior." *Journal of Marketing Research* 38, no. 3, pp. 281–295.

Brown, J.J. and P.H. Reingen. 1987. "Social Ties and Word-of-Mouth Referral Behavior." *Journal of Consumer Research* 14, no. 3, pp. 350–362. http://search.ebscohost.com/login.aspx?direct=true&db=bth&AN=4657957&site=ehost-live.

Bughin, J. 2015. "Getting a Sharper Picture of Social Media's Influence." *McKinsey Quarterly*. www.mckinsey.com/business-functions/marketing-and-sales/our-insights/getting-a-sharper-picture-of-social-medias-influence.

Bump, P. 2022. "The Marketing Trends of 2022." *Hubspot*. Retrieved from https://blog.hubspot.com/marketing/marketing-trends.

CFI Group. 2020. "Contact Center Satisfaction Index (CCSI)." *CFI Group*. Retrieved from https://cdncom.cfigroup.com/wp-content/uploads/CFI-contact-center-satisfaction-2020.pdf.

Confessore, N. April 04, 2018. "Cambridge Analytica and Facebook: The Scandal and the Fallout So Far." *The New York Times*. Retrieved from www.nytimes.com/2018/04/04/us/politics/cambridge-analytica-scandal-fallout.html.

C-SPAN. 2020. "Facebook and Twitter CEOs Testify on Regulating Social Media Content." *C-SPAN*. Retrieved from www.c-span.org/video/?478048-1/facebook-twitter-ceos-testify-regulating-social-media-content#.

Dembosky. April 2012. "In the West We're Mostly Social Media 'Lurkers.'" *The Globe and Mail*. www.theglobeandmail.com/technology/digital-culture/social-web/in-the-west-were-mostly-social-media-lurkers/article1357516/ (accessed February 08, 2017).

Fleming, G. 2016. "The Data Digest: Forrester's Social Technographics 2016." *Data Insights Professionals Blog*. http://blogs.forrester.com/category/social_technographics.

Gilly, M., J.L. Graham, M. Wolfinbarger, and L. Yale. 1998. "A Dyadic Study of Interpersonal Information Search." *The Journal of the Academy of Marketing Science* 26, no. 2, pp. 83–100.

Gong, W., E.P. Lim, and F. Zhu. 2015. "Characterizing Silent Users in Social Media Communities." In *Proceedings of the Ninth International AAAI Conference on Web and Social Media*, pp. 140–149.

Gramlich, J. 2021. "10 Facts About Americans and Facebook." *Pew Research Center*. Retrieved from www.pewresearch.org/fact-tank/2021/06/01/facts-about-americans-and-facebook/.

GWI. 2021. "Social Media Marketing in 2021." *Global WebIndex*. Retrieved from www.gwi.com/reports/social-report-b.

GWI. 2022. "The Biggest Social Media Trends for Social." *Global WebIndex*. Retrieved from www.gwi.com/reports/social.

Heath, A. October 25, 2021. "Facebook's Lost Generation." *The Verge*. Retrieved from www.theverge.com/22743744/facebook-teen-usage-decline-frances-haugen-leaks.

Herhold, K. 2019. "How People Interact on Social Media in 2019." *The Manifest Blog*. Retrieved from https://themanifest.com/social-media/how-people-interact-social-media.

Horwitz, J. September 13, 2021. "Facebook Says Its Rules Apply to All. Company Documents Reveal a Secret Elite That's Exempt." *The Wall Street Journal*. Retrieved from www.wsj.com/articles/facebook-files-xcheck-zuckerberg-elite-rules-11631541353?mod=series_facebookfiles.

Hsu, T. and E. Lutz. August 01, 2020. "More Than 1,000 Companies Boycotted Facebook. Did It Work?" *The New York Times*. Retrieved from www.nytimes.com/2020/08/01/business/media/facebook-boycott.html.

Influencer Marketing Hub. 2022. "The State of Influencer Marketing 2022." *Influencer Marketing Hub*. Retrieved from https://influencermarketinghub.com/ebooks/Influencer_Marketing_Benchmark_Report_2022.pdf.

Jones, K. 2016. "Motivations for Sharing on Facebook." *Fractl Blog*. Retrieved from https://blog.frac.tl/motivations-sharing-facebook.

Kang, C. September 30, 2021. "Facebook Grilled by Senators Over Its Effect on Children." *The New York Times*. Retrieved from www.nytimes.com/2021/09/30/technology/facebook-senate-hearing.html.

Li, C. 2010. *Open Leadership: How Social Technology Can Transform the Way You Lead*. New York, NY: John Wiley & Sons, Inc.

Mitchell, A. and M. Walker. 2021. "More Americans Now Say Government Should Take Steps to Restrict False Information Online Than in 2018." *Pew Research Center*. Retrieved from www.pewresearch.org/fact-tank/2021/08/18/more-americans-now-say-government-should-take-steps-to-restrict-false-information-online-than-in-2018/.

Mixon, I. 2016. "8 Statistics That Will Change the Way You Think About Referral Marketing." *Ambassador*. http://app.mhb.io/e/npo3/57 (accessed February 08, 2017).

Nanji, A. 2019. "Why People Follow (And Unfollow) Brands on Social Media." MarketingProfs. www.marketingprofs.com/charts/2019/41243/why-people-follow-and-unfollow-brands-on-social-media.

New York State Department of Financial Services. 2020. "Twitter Investigation Report." Retrieved from www.dfs.ny.gov/Twitter_Report.

Nielsen, J. 2006. *The 90-9-1 Rule for Participation Inequality in Social Media and Online Communities*. California: Nielsen Norman Group.

Park, C. and T.M. Lee. 2009. "Information Direction, Website Reputation and the eWOM Effect: A Moderating Role of Product Type." *Journal of Business Research* 62, no. 1, pp. 61–67.

Perrin, A. September 05, 2018. "Americans Are Changing Their Relationship With Facebook." Pew Research Center. Retrieved from www.pewresearch.org/fact-tank/2018/09/05/americans-are-changing-their-relationship-with-facebook/.

Perrin, A. June 03, 2021. "Mobile Technology and Home Broadband 2021." *Pew Research Center*. Retrieved from www.pewresearch.org/internet/2021/06/03/mobile-technology-and-home-broadband-2021/.

Pew Research Center. 2021a. "Social Media Fact Sheet." *Pew Research Center*. Retrieved from www.pewresearch.org/internet/fact-sheet/social-media/.

Pew Research Center. 2021b. "Mobile Fact Sheet." *Pew Research Center*. Retrieved from www.pewresearch.org/internet/fact-sheet/mobile/.

Richins, M. and P. Bloch. 1986. "After the New Wears Off: The Temporal Context of Product Involvement." *Journal of Consumer Research* 13, no. 2, pp. 280–285.

Schaeffer, K. 2021. "7 Facts About Americans and Instagram." *Pew Research Center*. Retrieved from www.pewresearch.org/fact-tank/2021/10/07/7-facts-about-americans-and-instagram/.

Scheck, J., N. Purnell, and J. Horwitz. September 16, 2021. "Facebook Employees Flag Drug Cartels and Human Traffickers—The Company's Response Is Weak, Documents Show." *The Wall Street Journal*. Retrieved from www.wsj.com/articles/facebook-drug-cartels-human-traffickers-response-is-weak-documents-11631812953?mod=series_facebookfiles.

Slama, M. and A. Tashcian. 1985. "Selected Socioeconomic and Demographic Characteristics Associated With Purchasing Involvement." *Journal of Marketing* 49, pp. 72–82.

Sprout Social. 2021. "The Future of Social Media: New Data for 2021 & Beyond." Sprout Social. Retrieved from https://sproutsocial.com/insights/data/harris-insights-report/.

Swant, M. 2016. "Twitter Says Users Now Trust Influencers Nearly as Much as Their Friends." *Adweek*. Retrieved from www.adweek.com/news/technology/twitter-says-users-now-trust-influencers-nearly-much-their-friends-171367.

The New York Times. 2011. "The Psychology of Sharing." Retrieved from https://foundationinc.co/wp-content/uploads/2018/12/NYT-Psychology-Of-Sharing.pdf.

The Washington Post. December 22, 2021. "November 4–22, Washington Post-Scholar School Tech Poll." Retrieved from www.washingtonpost.com/context/nov-4-22-2021-washington-post-schar-school-tech-poll/1f827037-688f-4030-a3e4-67464014a846/?itid=lk_inline_manual_6.

United States House. January 13, 2022. "Select Committee Subpoenas Social Media Companies for Records Related to January 6th Attack." Press Release January 6th Committee. Retrieved from https://january6th.house.gov/news

/press-releases/select-committee-subpoenas-social-media-companies-records-related-january-6th.

Vision Critical. 2014. "New Vision Critical Report Identifies Major Gaps in Social Media Data Companies Use to Analyze Customer Behavior." www.businesswire.com/news/home/20141209005233/en/New-Vision-Critical-Report-Identifies-Major-Gaps-in-Social-Media-Data-Companies-Use-to-Analyze-Customer-Behavior.

Wagner, K. and D. McLaughlin. October 25, 2021. "Facebook, Alarmed by Teen Usage Drop, Left Investors in the Dark." *Bloomberg*. Retrieved from www.bloomberg.com/news/articles/2021-10-25/facebook-files-show-growth-struggles-as-young-users-in-u-s-decline.

Walton, A. January 09, 2018. "Investors Pressure Apple Over Psychological Risks of Screen Time for Kids." *Forbes*. Retrieved from www.forbes.com/sites/alicegwalton/2018/01/09/investors-pressure-apple-over-psychological-risks-of-screen-time-for-kids/?sh=de10b9e38dfe.

Watt, N. 2016. "ADI: Best of the Best Brands Driving Social Media Success." *CMO*. www.cmo.com/adobe-digital-insights/articles/2016/7/18/adi-best-of-the-bestdriving-social-media-success-.html#gs.b90iG=k.

We Are Social and Hootsuite. 2021. "Digital 2021 Global Overview Report." Retrieved from https://wearesocial.com/uk/blog/2021/01/digital-2021-uk/.

We Are Social and Hootsuite. 2022. "Digital 2021 Global Overview Report." Retrieved from https://wearesocial.com/uk/blog/2022/01/digital-2022-another-year-of-bumper-growth-2/.

Webb, B. November 22, 2021. "Lush Is Quitting Social Media. The Start of a Trend?" *Vogue*. Retrieved from www.voguebusiness.com/consumers/lush-is-quitting-social-media-the-start-of-a-trend-facebook-instagram-snapchat-tiktok.

Wells, G., J. Horwitz, and D. Seetharaman. September 14, 2021. "Facebook Knows Instagram Is Toxic for Teen Girls, Company Documents Show." *The Wall Street Journal*. Retrieved from www.wsj.com/articles/facebook-knows-instagram-is-toxic-for-teen-girls-company-documents-show-11631620739?mod=series_facebookfiles.

Wood, Z. November 26, 2021. "'I'm Happy to Lose £10m by Quitting Facebook,' Says Lush Boss." *The Guardian*. Retrieved from www.theguardian.com/business/2021/nov/26/im-happy-to-lose-10m-by-quitting-facebook-says-lush-boss.

Woods, H. and H. Scott 2016. "#Sleepyteens: Social Media Use in Adolescence Is Associated With Poor Sleep Quality, Anxiety, Depression and Low Self-Esteem." *Journal of Adolescence* 51, pp. 41–49.

CHAPTER 3

Social Business

Technology has significantly transformed the business landscape over the last century. It has impacted not only how products and services are produced, marketed, and distributed but also how businesses communicate, build, and maintain a relationship with their consumers. Numerous technological advancements have strengthened and furthered the businesses' ability to grow and expand. For example, the Remington typewriter occupied a dominant presence in the workplace through most of the 1900s, and by the 1960s, the telephone displaced the traditional letter as the primary method of communication (Polt 1995; Dillerm 2015). The 1980s marked the beginning of the modern technology era with the introduction of the first personal computer (i.e., Apple's Macintosh), brick-size cellular phones, and the fax machine (Novell 2013). By the turn of the millennium, the rate of technological advancements exploded. The Internet led the charge. The Web made companies more accessible, e-mail became a popular communication tool, the first smartphone was released, we could send text and photo messages, and e-commerce changed forever the way we shop (Dillerm 2015; Williams 2012). Apple's iPhone introduction, coupled with high consumer-adoption rates of smartphones, further propelled the usage of social media and launched the era of the social consumer. Today, technology is fully integrated into all aspects of our daily lives. We live, work, and play in a digital world.

Historically, businesses held the majority of the power in the marketplace. Companies decided what to produce, when and where to release it, and how consumers would purchase and consume it. This is no longer true; today consumers sit in the driver's seat. Social media has given consumers a loud voice. They are now able to widely broadcast what they want, how, when, and where they want it. Consumers wield this power through their desktops or laptops, but more likely, through a small, powerful device that sits nicely in the palm of their hand. When consumers have a question, a complaint, or a compliment, they turn to their smartphone and share it with hundreds, thousands, and maybe even millions of other consumers on social media. If a company cannot give them what they want, they discount them with a swipe of their finger or the click of a button. The balance of power has shifted. For those companies slow to recognize this shift, the global health threat of late 2019 and early 2020 was a wake-up call.

The COVID-19 pandemic brought about the realization that every business is a technology business. In the United States, the average number of minutes spent on social networks rose by 16 percent (Statista 2020). As the world closed down and consumer mobility reduced, people naturally gravitated toward online channels. Companies recognized the importance of investing in digital technologies for internal operations, customer, and supply–chain interactions. A global study by management consultants McKinsey & Company (2020) of 899 c-suite executives and senior managers revealed that the pandemic accelerated the digitalization of customer interactions by an average of three years. Survey respondents indicated that upward of 80 percent of their customer interactions are now digital. Furthermore, business adoption of partial or fully digitized products and services to meet consumer expectations was accelerated by seven years. Not surprisingly, acceleration was more significant in some industries than others, with the most considerable growth seen in healthcare and pharma, financial and professional services (McKinsey & Company 2020). Once consumers have developed a taste for digital interaction, they are often unwilling to return to the old methods. Therefore, we can expect consumer needs and expectations for digital technologies and exchanges, including the use of social media, to remain in a post-COVID world.

For a company to succeed today, they need to embrace the power of social media, to make it part of who they are and what they do. Companies need to evolve into social businesses. Those who fail to make this transition may find themselves left behind. As a wise person once said, companies must innovate or die. Innovation is not just about new product development; it is also about developing new ways of doing business. In this chapter, we will explain what it means to be a social business and why it is crucial for your company to embrace this change. We will also explain the stages of social business development and how social tools can be integrated to become part of your company's DNA. Interspersed throughout the chapter are examples of companies that have successfully made the transition. Hopefully, they will inspire you to do the same.

The Social Business

Social business is "activities that use social media, social software and social networks to enable efficient, effective and mutually useful connections between people, information, and assets" (Kiron 2012). When a company becomes a social business, they no longer view social media solely as a marketing or public relations communication tool but as a tool that can be used throughout various strategic, innovative, and functional areas of a company. The COVID-19 pandemic has demonstrated the need for accelerated social media adoption to sustain and grow businesses. The transition is not easy; it requires leadership, resources, and time.

Social Business Maturity Model

The social business maturity model presented in Table 3.1 was developed from a combination of academic frameworks and industry models.

Trial Phase

The trial phase of social business is not unlike Hollywood's portrayal of the Wild West, chaotic and lawless. In this phase, social media is not a formal part of the business. Company social media accounts are often created in silos, functioning independently from other company social media accounts. Those that exist were created by individual departments or social-savvy and (in some cases) not-so-socially savvy employees. These accounts were more than likely created without undergoing a formal approval process. There may be duplicate accounts, inconsistent posting and engagement practices, and unauthorized or inappropriate use of company intellectual property (e.g., logos, trademarks). During this phase, there is no strategy or goals in place. There is little synergy between accounts. Your company may be using social media as a broadcasting

Table 3.1 Social business maturity model

	Trial	Transition	Maturity
Current status	• No clear goals • No formal policy • No plan • No control • Ad hoc and experimental social initiatives • Using social media as a broadcasting channel	• More focused activities • Allocation of some resources • Movement from listening to engaging with consumers • Social media is primarily used for marketing and PR purposes • Some, but inconsistent interaction with consumers	• Social media monitoring • Communicating feedback • Employee, consumer, and influencer engagement • More focused use of social media in a number of functional areas
Next steps	• Learn how your consumers use social media • Listen to what they are saying • Conduct a competitive audit • Develop, implement, and learn from pilot projects • Prioritize initiatives	• Creation of a Social Media Advisory Board or Center of Excellence • Policy formation and rules for engagement • Goal alignment with strategic business goals • Encourage employee engagement • Providing employee support and training • Identifying social influencers • Exploration of how social media can be used in other functional areas—HR, Sales, Finance, and so on • Measuring and communicating results • Ongoing monitoring	• Obtaining C-level support and engagement • Social media moves into all areas of the business—HR, Sales, Finance, and so on • Social media is now part of the business planning process • Policies and procedures updated to allow for companywide participation • Review Advisory Board or Center of Excellence role and composition
Resources required	• Obtaining support from senior management • Human resources • Identify social media evangelists • Listening or monitoring platform	• Allocation of additional human resources • Social media management system	• Ongoing education and support

Source: Adapted from van Luxemburg (2011), Li and Solis (2013), Effing and Spil (2016). The model describes three phases of social business. It identifies activities that typically take place during each phase, the steps and the resources required to move your company to the next phase.

channel—posting the same information on each platform instead of customizing information for each platform and using specific platforms to engage consumers in conversation and build relationships. Your company may not have a social media policy that outlines what employees can and cannot post. Your employees are often unaware of the laws and regulations that they are required to be followed. Sometimes, the intern(s) is solely charged with crafting your company's social media presence (Tip: Don't do this). In this phase, the mindset is "let's give it a shot and see what happens."

Chaos aside, there is value in experimentation. However, this value will go unrealized if no one pays careful attention. Social businesses need to listen and learn. So, let's get a little more focused. There are at least four valuable sources of information you can draw upon to learn about how to use social media for business purposes: (1) publicly available information, (2) information about your social media connections, (3) information about your current consumer base, and (4) information about your competition.

Public Information

The beauty (and curse) of social media is that it is constantly growing and evolving. Platforms that were once popular (e.g., MySpace) lose their appeal and are replaced with other platforms (e.g., Facebook). New platforms are launched and become hugely successful (e.g., Instagram and Snapchat), others transform by adding new features (e.g., Pinterest), and some simply fail to catch on (e.g., Gowalla). How consumers use and engage with social media also changes. A decade ago, social media was used primarily to connect with family and friends. Today, as we learned in Chapter 2, consumers use it for various additional purposes, such as to meet new people, be inspired, research products, catch up on the latest news, find employment, and be entertained. Social media has certainly come a long way. Strategies that worked well on social media five years ago may not work well today. Companies need to keep up-to-date on the growth and popularity of different platforms and understand how consumers are currently using them. Fortunately, there is ample publicly available information on this topic. Pew Internet (pewinternet.

org), eMarketer (emarketer.com), Social Media Examiner (socialmediaexaminer.com), Nielsen (nielsen.com), Forrester (forrester.com), and McKinsey (mckinsey.com) are all excellent places to start.

Social Connections

The key to marketing success is by understanding your consumers. This truism is no different in the social space. Therefore, you need to learn as much as you can from your existing social connections. To begin, select a sample of 20 to 30 of your social media followers and review their accounts to see when they use social (day and time), how frequently they use it (frequency of posts), and what type of content they appear to be interested in (evident by status updates, shares, likes, comments, and so on). You are likely to find that there are platform differences in how consumers are using and engaging with your brand. For example, consumers may be more active on Facebook than on Twitter. They may like watching the videos you share on Facebook but do not engage with those you post to Twitter. Next, examine your social accounts carefully to see what type of content resonates the strongest with your followers. Look for content that receives the greatest level of engagement from your followers (i.e., likes, shares, comments, retweets). Take note of specific content that fails to ignite a response. A final step is to conduct a sentiment analysis, a process by which you perform a keyword search, typically your company name to see what people are saying about your company across social media. Sentiment analysis also quantifies and categorizes comments as positive, negative, and neutral. There is a large number of free and fee-based sentiment analysis services available: Social Mention (socialmention.com—free), WhosTalkin (whostalkin.com—free), HowSocialable (howsocialable.com—fee-based), Mention (mention.com—fee-based), and Keyhole.co (keyhole.co-fee-based). These will allow you not only to see what people are saying about your company, brand, product, competition, or industry in real time but also help you determine if they like you.

Consumer Base

While social media can provide a valuable window into the lives of your consumers, you may still need a better view. If you need more information on your consumers' social media habits, then it is a good idea to survey them. A formal survey can be drafted and distributed via e-mail or social media. Alternatively, you could add a couple of questions to an existing task (e.g., order form) or interaction (e.g., customer service call). An informal, exploratory survey format using social media is another option. A company could simply ask or post a question on Twitter or Facebook and document consumer feedback.

Competition

There is a lot that you can learn about how to and how not to use social media by simply monitoring the social activities of your competitors. Identify three or more competitors to monitor. Select the industry leader and a couple of your immediate competitors and audit their social media activities. Identify which platforms they use, how active they are on each platform, how they use their brand voice, how they embody their brand story (more on this later), what they post, and the kind of response these posts generate. Try to identify the content and timing of posts that work for each platform. Similarly, identify what does not appear to work. In other words, what posts did not generate much consumer engagement (i.e., likes, retweets, comments)? You can learn just as much from their failures as you can from their successes.

To monitor your consumers' and your competitors' social media habits, it may be worthwhile to purchase a subscription to a social media monitoring platform. There are myriad of options available depending on the amount and level of data you wish to capture and the size of your budget. Getting into the nuances of social media monitoring is beyond the scope of this book, but a low-cost and effective option to start with is Hootsuite (hootsuite.com). Other commonly used options include Sprout Social, Meltwater, and Cyfe.

Once you have observed and learned as much as you can from your connections, consumers, and competitors, you will be able to formulate a set of assumptions about the best way to generate a following and successfully engage with your consumers on social media to encourage social word of mouth (sWOM). Now it is time to test some of these assumptions. Pick one or two social media accounts, and over a period of a couple of weeks, pilot these assumptions. Monitor each and every post to determine success. After a couple of weeks of experimenting with different approaches, you will be ready to prioritize future initiatives. Remember, the goal is quality, not quantity. It is better to have a small number of well-executed initiatives on a couple of social media platforms that generate positive results than it is to try and be everywhere and do everything. In other words, do not jump into simultaneously creating a Facebook, Twitter, Instagram, YouTube, and TikTok account. Take, for example, Apple; they are very active on Instagram but surprisingly quiet on other platforms. Be realistic about what you can achieve, given the resources you have at your disposal. Your holistic social media efforts are a marathon and not a sprint.

There are two primary social media resources you will need: financial resources for a monitoring service subscription as well as any resources required for your initiatives (i.e., content generation and organization) and human resources to develop, implement, and monitor your pilot projects. During this phase, social media responsibilities largely fall to the marketing department. Someone in the marketing department needs to be assigned the responsibility of managing the company's social media initiatives—a Director of Social Media or Social Media Manager. To assist this person now and in the future, it is essential that you identify and recruit social media evangelists—employees at all levels of the organization who recognize the importance of social media as a business tool. These evangelists can be very influential at gaining companywide support, beginning at the senior level.

Executive Buy-In

Executive buy-in and support are essential for success (Kiron 2012). C-level executives differ in their perceptions of social media and the importance and value of creating a social business. There are many reasons why executives are often reluctant to adopt social, including the perception that the investment may be worth the time, particularly if existing traditional media is working. They may feel that social media in the hands of employees is risky and the reward is minimal. This is a valid concern, but employee education and training can mitigate many risks. They may think their target market is not using social media. This may have been the case 10 years ago, but it is hard to argue this point today. As we learned in Chapter 2, consumer social media adoption rates have changed dramatically over the years. In 2021, 73 percent of US consumers aged 50 to 64 and 65 percent of those aged 65+ used at least one social media platform, up from 69 to 40 percent, respectively, in 2019 (Pew Research Center 2021).

Transition Phase

The transition phase is the evolutionary phase. Having completed the steps of listening and learning, conducting a competitive audit, and piloting initiatives, it is time to put all of this knowledge to good use. During the transition phase, social media activities become more focused. Instead of trying to do it all and be something for everyone, the company directs its social media efforts toward specific consumer groups and social platforms. There is a movement from listening to consumers to engaging with them. Resource allocation has improved but likely has room to grow. To gain support for additional resources, it is important for you to keep monitoring, measuring, and reporting results. Senior management needs to see that social media is worth the investment. Now may be an appropriate time to acquire or trade up to a more robust social media monitoring and management system. Hootsuite may continue to be a good long-term option for small-to-medium-size companies. Larger companies may eventually need to upgrade to a more sophisticated system with additional features. Social monitoring leaders include Salesforce, Sysomos, Visual Technologies, and Viral Heat.

When the focus becomes engagement, it is time to establish a social media advisory board. An advisory board or a center of excellence is a group of individuals whose purpose is to craft a company social media policy and provide appropriate guidelines for using social media in the workplace. We cover social media policies and advisory boards in Chapter 7.

Employee Engagement

The primary reason why many companies adopt social media is to connect with and motivate external consumers. This is a legitimate reason but do not forget your internal consumers—your employees. Social media can build and maintain business relationships between employees and between employees and senior management. Social media can be an effective communication channel for sharing company news and fostering a sense of company pride.

In their book, *The Social Employee,* authors Cheryl and Mark Burgess stress that the primary drivers of social business are employees (Burgess and Burgess 2014). They are right. Your employees are the face of your company, engaging with consumers and the public daily. It will be challenging to succeed as a social business without employee support. Company employees are "low-hanging fruit" when it comes to increasing your social media following. Employees have expertise that can be shared on social media and may be very helpful in spreading positive sWOM. Through social media, employees can foster long-term relationships with social consumers. Empowering your employees to share company information on their personal accounts may make your company more accessible to people outside of your company network.

In truth, not all employees are socially savvy, especially about how to use social media for business purposes. Some employees may also be reluctant to take on additional social responsibilities. To build a culture of collaboration and social sharing among your employees, you need to identify your social media evangelists and perhaps create a social media employee advocacy program. An employee advocate is someone who represents the interests of the company to internal and external audiences. These employees may be product or service experts, perhaps partly because of their position within the company and, therefore, a perceived credible spokesperson for the company. In other cases, they may be actively engaged with and have large social media networks that represent valuable contacts for the company. These employees can individually and collectively help promote the company and specific products and services through their social media accounts. Companies that have successfully implemented employee advocacy programs include Dell (computers), Kelly Services (staffing agency), Zappos (E-commerce), and Starbucks (retail). In Chapter 5, we will discuss the process of creating and managing an employee advocacy program.

Integrating Social Throughout the Company

The chances are that your company is using social media primarily for marketing and public relations purposes. This is great, but the deep integration of social media into multiple areas of the organization is necessary to transform your company into a social business. It is time to start exploring opportunities for incorporating social throughout the company.

The following section provides a brief overview of how social media can add value to a company and increase company-related sWOM.

Strategic Insights and Execution

Social media can help business leaders by offering strategic insights and improving strategic execution. In the case of strategic insights, a company can analyze consumer comments and perform brand sentiment analysis to identify problems with existing products and anticipate shifts in consumer preferences. In 2017, Taco Bell was ranked number five on Fast Company's most innovative social media companies. Instead of relying solely on traditional marketing research techniques such as surveys and focus groups, the company listens to its 20+ million consumers. Customer service is a top priority for the company. When they learned through social media that consumers were unhappy with the cheese in their Quesalupa, they reached out to restaurants to remind them to follow the recipe to ensure quality control (Gorbatch 2019).

Comments can live online forever. Positive comments help consumers evaluate products, make purchase decisions, and reaffirm their selection. This helps with product sales and brand reputation. However, when a complaint or criticism is shared on social media, it has the potential to do harm. After a comment is posted, it moves from a private matter to a public one. The source of the complaint will determine the impact that it will have on the brand's reputation and sales. When the complaint comes from a consumer, who has a high number of social connections, and if these social connections are not closely connected to each other, there is the potential for a firestorm (Stich, Golla, and Nanopoulos 2014). A firestorm is a "sudden discharge of large quantities of messages containing negative WOM and complaint behavior against a person, company, or group in social media networks" (Pfeffer, Zorbach, and Carley 2014, 118). In other words, negativity may breed negativity. Recipients or readers of the complaint may contribute to the conversation by voicing or sharing the initial complaint with their social networks. For this reason, companies need to have a strategy for handling the negative sWOM.

Innovation

Social media can be a great tool for solving problems with existing products and sourcing ideas for new ones. By listening to online conversations, Netflix learned that many people fall asleep while binge-watching their favorite shows. The entertainment company saw this as an opportunity to create a new product—Netflix Socks. These smart socks can detect when the viewer is nodding off and signal the television to pause the show. Now we won't wake up only to realize that we have slept through three episodes or that our hero has met an untimely death! Fitbit uses social listening to identify emerging issues and troubleshoot problems with its activity tracker. The company collects all of the ideas generated by the users to bring to their engineering team for review. One great example that originated from social listening was creating the "Reminders to Move" feature—a buzzing sensation initiated by the wrist device to encourage users to get up and move (Gorbatch 2019). Personal care brand, Nivea, assumed that when it came to purchasing deodorant, consumers were most concerned about skin irritations and length of protection. However, when the company analyzed social media comments about the brand, they learned that consumers were most concerned about the stains on their clothes caused by the deodorant's residue. Nivea used these insights to create a new product—Nivea Invisible for Black and White.

Human Resources

If you have been employed in the same position for a while, you may not realize how the recruitment process has changed. Help wanted ads and paper resumes are artifacts of yesteryear—say "hello" to social recruiting. Social recruiting is using popular social media platforms to advertise, source, and recruit potential candidates for a job. In 2020, 92 percent of employers surveyed reported using social and professional networks to recruit. The same survey revealed that 86 percent of job seekers used social media to search, apply to, or engage with employment-related social media content or reach out to recruiters (PR Newswire 2021).

A study by The Harris Poll revealed that 71 percent of US hiring decision makers agree that social media profiles are an effective way to screen potential candidates. Seventy percent of survey respondents believe that employers should be using social media profiles to screen candidates. Fifty-five percent report finding content on personal social media accounts that caused them not to hire the candidate. Checking a publicly available social media account can assist in validating work history and experience. It can also eliminate potential candidates if social posts indicate that the beliefs and value systems of the candidate do not align with those of the company (PR Web 2020). With over 722 million members, LinkedIn is the most popular platform for searching for candidates, with over 90 percent of recruiters using the platform for this purpose. Whereas membership spans all age groups, 59.9 percent of members are aged 25 to 34 years, suggesting it is a prime target to find and attract entry-level college graduates. Over 40 million people use LinkedIn to search for jobs each week (Newberry 2021). Despite the popularity and benefits of social recruiting, care should be taken when using social media or other Internet search tools to vet job applicants. Information obtained through social media may be outdated, inaccurate, unreliable, or protected by Title VII of the Civil Rights Act of 1964. Title VII prohibits employment discrimination based on race, color, religion, sex, and national origin. This information is typically omitted from a resume and job application form but may be inadvertently obtained while viewing the applicant's social media account (Global HR Research 2015).

Marketing Communications

Social media is first and foremost a communication channel. It is a channel that provides a two-way dialog between consumers, between a company and its consumers, and between companies. Social media is a conversation tool. It allows you to communicate with consumers by either broadcasting a general message or delivering a personalized, individual message. Broadcasting is akin to a megaphone—a company reaches a large number of people with a single message (mass communication). The company crafts a message and talks to the consumer, not unlike the traditional mass media (TV, radio, and print). The difference, however, between traditional and social media is the timeliness of the communication. Social media allows immediate access and real-time communication with your consumers at a fraction of the cost of traditional media.

Broadcasting general messages to your entire network may be appropriate some of the time but certainly not all of the time. On social media, you have a direct line to your consumers, much like a telephone. You should use this opportunity to engage specific segments of your network and individual consumers in conversations. Thus, your social media efforts should consist of a combination of mass and targeted and personalized communications.

> The best way to sell a product is not to sell it at all.

Companies should not view social media as purely a sales channel, but as an important contributor to the consumer decision-making process. In truth, the best way to sell a product is not to sell it at all. Instead, a good sales representative will have a conversation with you, she or he asks questions, listens, and provides guidance. Social media allows companies to have one-on-one conversations with individual consumers. It is like chatting with someone on the telephone. As a company engages in a conversation with a specific consumer, other social media users can eavesdrop and may even chime in on the conversation. The conversation may eventually lead to a sale. During the COVID-19 pandemic, many businesses experienced a drastic drop in revenues. In response, they utilized social media to generate awareness, enhance their brand identity, and maintain their connections with consumers. For instance, many hotels initially experienced up to a 50 percent drop in revenues due to travel restrictions. Silverado Resort and Spa amended its digital strategy to focus on educating the consumer about personal well-being. They created and shared several posts that explained how different plants could help boost immunity. Ikea encouraged consumers to stay positive, keep safe, and find comfort in their homes. Nike urged fans to "Play inside, play for the world" (Anand n.d.). In Chapters 4 and 6, we will talk more about how to have conversations with consumers by crafting persuasive social media messages.

Humanizing the Brand

Consumers respond positively to brands that represent who they are or whom they want to be. Have you ever heard yourself say something to the effect of "Yes, it (insert brand name) is nice, but it's just not me?" If the answer is yes, then you may be saying that the personality of the brand is not consistent with your identity. When consumers choose to follow and engage with a brand on social media, they do so because they identify with the brand. As we discussed in Chapter 2, this is a motivating factor in why we share. Consumers see their real or aspirational sense of self (i.e., whom they want to be) reflected in the brand. Once they follow the brand on social media, the brand becomes part of their online social identity. This brand association becomes one of the many important data points connected to a consumer's profile(s). Collectively, this information paints a picture of a consumer's social identity that is broadcasted across the social media network(s). You are whom you like. The brand and consumer social identity association provide numerous benefits such as increasing brand awareness, extending your communication reach, and increasing the consumer's brand involvement. It may also increase consumer engagement, stimulate sWOM, improve the reputation of your company, drive traffic to your website, and improve your search engine ranking. To encourage consumers to make this connection, a company needs to humanize their brand.

To humanize your brand is to imagine your brand as it were a person, to give your brand a personality—a set of traits that people attribute to your product as if it were a real person (Aaker, Vohs, and Mogilner 2010). A brand personality makes your brand more relatable and helps to distinguish it from the competition. The greater the congruence between a brand's personality and the real or aspirational personality of the consumer, the stronger the preference for the brand (Aaker 1997). If your brand were a person, how would you describe its personality? Are they formal or relaxed? Feisty or timid? Conservative or progressive? Innovative or conventional? Energetic or easy-going? If you are uncertain, look at your brand values for guidance.

Brand Voice

Once you have determined your brand personality, you then need to develop your brand voice. That is, you need to decide not only the types of content that you will share but also *how* you will communicate with consumers on social media. Brand voice is an important way in which your company can stand out from the crowded digital landscape. Whereas visual content such as your logo, graphics, and videos are essential, so too is your written content. Your brand voice is the personality that your brand takes on in communications and includes the words, phrases, and stylistic choices you use in your messaging. In a study performed by Sprout Social, 33 percent of respondents indicated that a distinct personality helped make a brand stand out (Chen 2020). The process of developing a distinctive brand voice begins with reviewing your company's mission and values. This will help you identify appropriate personality traits and appropriate language and tone. Next, you should conduct an audit of your current voice on social media. Are the tone, language, phrases, and stylistic choices consistent with the personality you are trying to portray? If not, what changes may be necessary? Consider your target audience(s). What is their demographic profile, which social media do they use, and why? How do they speak on social media? What vocabulary and tone will they find appealing and will match your brand? For example, fast-casual restaurant, Smashburger is unlikely to post content related to the virtues of a vegetarian diet or low-fat food. Instead, they celebrate "holidays" such as National Bacon Lovers Day (FYI: It's August 20). If your company is very formal then when replying to consumer posts, you may decide to address the consumer by their last name (e.g., Mr. Jones). On the other hand, if your company is very informal and spontaneous, you may choose to share witty content and use the consumer's first names (e.g., Hi Bob!).

Some examples of companies with strong and distinct brand voices include Taco Bell, Intel, and Adidas (Figures 3.1–3.6).

Figure 3.1 Taco Bell Twitter example 1

Figure 3.2 Taco Bell Twitter example 2
Source: Images courtesy of Taco Bell's public Twitter account.

Taco Bell's personality and brand voice could be described as humorous and somewhat wacky.

Step into an ocean of inspiration with the interactive Electric Jellyfish installation. With the help of Intel tech, visitors can shoot, wobble, and bounce light with the touch of a finger. http://intel.ly/29VGvXf

Figure 3.3 Intel's Facebook example 1

With fitness junkies craving insights, motivation and praise, companies are eager to oblige. Check out these 7 wacky wearables that go way beyond the typical fitness tracker: http://intel.ly/29QBkI3

Figure 3.4 Intel's Facebook example 2
Source: Images courtesy of Intel's public Facebook page.

Intel's voice is smart and enlightening.

Figure 3.5 Adidas Twitter example 1

adidas @adidas · Jun 8
Today we start a journey to save the oceans.
Support @Parleyxxx's Ocean Plastic Program.
Create a movement.

Figure 3.6 Adidas Twitter example 2
Source: Images courtesy of Adidas public Twitter account.

Adidas is inspirational.

Once you have developed your voice, you will need to provide guidelines for your employees to follow, guidelines on acceptable content, and manner of speech. Employees and third parties who are authorized to post on behalf of the company will need direction to ensure a consistent brand voice, which is essential for presenting an accurate and consistent brand identity. You do not want Jim in accounting to be super serious, Jenny in human resources to be feisty, and your social media influencers or paid endorsers to be totally irreverent. Consider creating a brand voice style guide, a document that offers a description of your personality traits and gives examples of appropriate language and tone. This brand voice style guide should form part of your company's social media policies and procedures documentation.

It is also important to meet periodically with your social media team to review whether or not your social media posts are consistent with your brand voice. Find emblematic social media posts and examples of consumer engagement that embody the essence of your brand. It is also helpful to pinpoint posts that are not consistent with your brand and identify the reasons why (i.e., word choice, tone, subject matter). And it goes without saying, learn from your social media mistakes (there will be many!). Archive and revisit these positive and negative examples.

Customer Service

If you had a question about a recent purchase, how would you contact the company? Would you call them on the 1–800 number? Jump in your car and head to the store? Try the live chat feature on their website? Perhaps, you would send them a tweet? Or, post a question on the company's Facebook page? Maybe you would not contact the company. Perhaps, you would post a message on social media and let members of your social network respond. Social customer service or s-Care is the delivery of customer service via social networks rather than call centers, retail stores, service counters, and company websites. Upward of 80 percent of consumers use social to engage with brands (Fontanella 2020). Some of the engagement includes asking for help. Perhaps not surprisingly, when it comes to seeking assistance, there are generational differences. Thirty-one percent of Zoomers (born 1997–2012) and 29 percent of Millennials (born 1981–1996) report using social media platforms such as Facebook and Twitter to contact a company. This number drops to 10 percent for those aged 55+ who still favor traditional customer service channels. Zoomers are more likely to attempt to solve issues on their own. Three out of every four Zoomers report conducting online research (e.g., comparing brands and reading reviews) before they buy, and 30 percent said they attempted to solve issues on their own before reaching out for assistance (Grieve 2021).

Tolerance of poor customer service also varies by generation. Fifty-three percent of Millennials and 34 percent of Zoomers said they are likely to switch to a competitor after one poor customer service experience, suggesting that (at least for now) young consumers are more likely to tolerate a single bad experience. It is only after multiple negative experiences that they are likely to switch to a competitor (64 percent). Wealth or lack thereof may be a contributing factor. Younger consumers have less spending power and shopping experience and are more likely to tolerate a poor service encounter than older, more experienced, and potentially wealthier consumers. When probed on what aspects of the customer experience negatively impacted their interaction, nearly half of the Zoomers respondents reported having to interact with an "unfriendly support agent." Helpful empathetic service agents are essential to this generation (Grieve 2021).

It is fair to say that the COVID-19 pandemic had a significant impact on customer service. Mandatory stay-at-home orders forced many consumers to turn to social media and digital technologies for assistance. Research suggests that of all generations, Zoomers followed by Millennials were most affected by the pandemic. Twenty-one percent of Zoomers and 20 percent of Millennials surveyed reported higher expectations for customer service during the pandemic than consumers aged 55+. Similarly, 18 percent of both Zoomers and Millennials reported becoming less patient during customer service interactions compared to 10 percent of older consumers (Grieve 2021).

By 2030, Millennials and Zoomers will be the two largest consumer groups in the United States (Grieve 2021). At this time, customer service via social media will no longer be an option for businesses; it will be a requirement. So why wait? If they have not already done so, consider offering customer service via social media. Here are some suggestions:

- When targeting a mix of generations, it is essential to select a combination of traditional, digital, and social media customer service channels.
- Create a dedicated handle for each social media service account (e.g., @TMobileHelp). This will ensure that requests for help are directed to the right person and can be answered faster.
- The bio/about section of the account should indicate the purpose of the account (e.g., global business support or customer support).
- The bio/about section should also communicate when live support is available. For example, "24/7 support 365 days" or "8 a.m.–8 p.m. Mon–Fri."
- Consider encouraging customer service representatives to sign off their posts on social media with their first names. This is a strategy that has been adopted by TMobile and can assist in humanizing the brand.

- Rather than looking for your dedicated customer support account, many customers will automatically visit your primary social media account. So be sure to provide the handle for the customer service account in the bio/about section (e.g., for customer service, visit @TMobileHelp).
- Consider including links on each social media account to FAQ documents/videos/websites to encourage self-service.
- Identify repeat questions and use these as an opportunity to update FAQs and create new resources.
- Provide those employees who manage the account with guidelines to ensure a consistent approach to handling questions and maintaining the appropriate brand voice. These guidelines should include a target response time for each new question, proper tone and language, and protocols for escalating issues or complaints.

Social media is not only important and effective for dealing with consumers directly, but it is also important for sharing information internally to help solve consumer problems. Take, for example, Nationwide Mutual Insurance Company. A Nationwide customer was stranded on vacation—his RV had broken down. He called the Nationwide call center for assistance—did his policy cover this situation? The call center agent was uncertain and decided to post the case on the company's internal social collaboration platform. People from all across the company chimed in to help solve the problem. Within 30 minutes, the call center representative had an answer and a detailed approach to help the customer. Without this internal social collaboration system, the problem may have taken hours or even days to resolve, and Nationwide could have lost a customer (Kiron 2012). Furthermore, unanswered questions, unresolved issues, and unreturned calls can often lead to negative WOM. It is not uncommon for dissatisfied consumers to turn to social media to publicly air their grievances. This has the potential to create a firestorm. Even if it does not motivate others to complain, it can still discourage consumers from doing business with your company.

Maturity Phase

During the maturity phase, the company's social media moves beyond marketing to include other functional areas. Policies and procedures may need to be updated, and the role and composition of the social media advisory board modified to accommodate the enhanced use of social media and to include representation from additional areas. Hopefully, all of the C-level executives now see the value of social. If some members of senior management are still wavering, it may be worthwhile to involve them with a specific social initiative that will help achieve one of their goals (Li and Solis 2013).

The key to determining if you have successfully made the transition to a social business is when social is an integral part of the business planning process and when there is companywide support and usage of social. Social is now part of the fabric of your business; it is part of the company's DNA.

An example of an organization that has successfully transitioned to a social business is the American Red Cross. The American Red Cross was founded in 1881 with the mission to "prevent and alleviate human suffering in the face of emergencies by mobilizing the power of volunteers and the generosity of donors" (American Red Cross 2021). To help them achieve their mission, the Red Cross made the commitment to infuse social media into every aspect of the organization. First and foremost, they have the commitment of senior management. Senior management recognizes the unique capabilities of social media to mobilize the masses to prepare for and respond to disasters.

The Red Cross operates accounts on a variety of social platforms, each with a specific purpose. To share the history of the company and to help build an emotional connection with the public, they use Facebook, LinkedIn, Instagram, TikTok, YouTube, and Twitter. Facebook is used primarily to connect with supporters, volunteers, blood donors, and others who are looking for information on the services provided. LinkedIn is where people can explore current job openings. Instagram is used to share photographs and videos of disaster relief responders in the field. TikTok offers safety tips, historical facts, and an inside look at life at the Red Cross. The Red Cross YouTube account informs the public about disaster response and helps to educate the public on topics such as CPR. Twitter is used for real-time updates on disasters and Red Cross services (Figure 3.7).

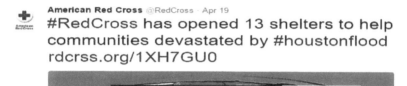

Figure 3.7 Red Cross Twitter example
Source: Image courtesy of Red Cross public Twitter account.

In addition to using social media to educate, communicate, and build relationships with supporters, the Red Cross also uses social media to make business decisions. By monitoring social chatter and public sentiment, they can identify how to respond to public needs. For example, by tracking keywords like "tornado" on Twitter, the Red Cross can spot exactly when and where disasters are happening and use this information to help manage and track resources and supplies.

Social is also an important tool for fundraising. Supporters can make a donation through one of their blogs or on Facebook. They use Twitter to post messages encouraging followers to donate to specific disasters (Kane 2014).

If a 140-year-old charitable organization with over 600 chapters, 20,000 employees, and 314,000 volunteers in the United States alone can make the commitment and transition to becoming a social business what is stopping your company?

Social B2B Companies

You may be thinking that social media is not particularly relevant to those companies that operate in the business-to-business (B2B) market. After all, who on earth would be interested in a photograph of your frontend loaders, sea containers, or enterprise software? But you would be surprised just how important social is to these companies. Research revealed that more than 80 percent of B2B decision makers at the C-level and VP-level across all industries admitted to being influenced by social media and at least 75 percent of B2B businesses use social media as part of their marketing strategy (Sagefrog Marketing Group 2021). A 2021 survey revealed that the top three social media platforms adopted by B2B marketers are Facebook (89 percent), LinkedIn (81 percent), and Instagram (72 percent) (Statista 2021). The following are some examples of B2B success on social media.

Maersk Group

The world's largest shipping container company with offices in 130 countries utilizes LinkedIn, Twitter, Facebook, Instagram, and YouTube to share news about the company to get closer to its consumers and potentially influence the industry (Katona and Sarvary 2014). Shipping enthusiasts are drawn to the company's posts and even post their photos of Maersk ships (Figure 3.7). By contributing their materials, these followers help to craft and share the story of Maersk throughout the social web (Katona and Sarvary 2014).

IBM

IBM uses social media to tell the 100+ year story of their company. Instagram is used to post photos and videos of employees sharing information about their personal experiences at IBM. Providing insights into new technologies helps promote the company values of trust, innovation, and responsibility (Morrison 2021).

Shopify

Ecommerce platform Shopify utilizes Facebook and YouTube to share How-To videos and tutorials for digital business owners. Their educational and entertaining content positions the company as a valuable resource for aspiring entrepreneurs (Morrison 2021).

Slack

Slack is a workplace communication and collaboration platform. The company uses Twitter to reach different audiences. In addition to creating their own content, they also share third-party articles on topics their customers may find appealing (Moreno 2020).

Airtable

Airtable is a cloud-based collaboration tool. The company uses Instagram to educate companies about its services and Instagram stories to showcase its brand personality. They regularly feature their employees and share behind-the-scenes and real-time in-the-moment content to humanize their brand (Moreno 2020).

In light of the influence of social media in the B2B market, we feel it is important to revisit some important facts for those readers who work for a B2B company:

> - Decision makers are on social media: Although the buying process in the B2B market is fundamentally different from the B2C market, purchase decision makers are more than likely on social media. This is a great way to reach and influence them.
> - Social media can help create brand awareness: Brand awareness is still very much a goal for B2B businesses. Other B2B companies are active on social media. Like traditional consumers, they will hear about your company through social media posts and your company's social media profiles.
> - Social media can build connections: Social media provides unique opportunities to not only research other companies but also to make connections with decision makers and industry influencers.
> - Social media can humanize your brand: B2B companies have a personality that also needs to be shared.
> - Social media can be used to help educate the public: You should take the opportunity to use social media to educate other companies (and consumers) on the importance of your product. While you may not be directly selling to

(Continues)

> consumers, if they perceive actual or real problems with your product, they can voice their concerns to others, which could create public relations problems.
> - Social media is not just for marketing: As we have seen in this chapter, social media can be infused throughout the entire company to connect people, information, and assets with the goal of making your company more efficient and competitive.

We conclude this chapter with one more example, the case of SAP. SAP is a B2B company that has successfully made the transition to becoming a social business.

SAP

Systems Applications and Products (SAP) is the market leader in enterprise software to help companies manage business operations and customer relations. Headquartered in Walldorf, Baden-Wurttemberg, Germany, SAP employs almost 102,000 people in 130 countries. SAP's vision is to "help the world run better and improve people's lives" (SAP 2016). They embedded social media into their organization for strategic insight and execution, innovation, human resources, marketing communications, and customer service. Like many other businesses, they have a wide selection of accounts on multiple platforms, including, Facebook, Twitter, YouTube, LinkedIn, and Instagram.

The most powerful illustration that SAP is a social business is the SAP Community Network, a global online community of over 2.8 million IT people, technologists, partners, business experts, students, professors, consultants, and influencers from more than 200 countries (SAP 2015). The community that is hosted by SAP includes blogs, wikis, and discussion forums. It is a place where members can discuss SAP products, programming languages, industries, and technology. How-to guides, white papers, and free downloads are all available on the site. Community members can post questions that are answered by either a company representative or other members of the community.

For a company to be successful in today's hyper-connected world, the company needs to embrace social media. sWOM begins internally; it begins with engaging with and empowering your employees to use social media for business purposes. Social media needs to be integrated into your company, much in the same way the telephone and the computer did decades ago. Social media is the telephone of this generation—ringing loudly and constantly. The question is, are you going to answer it?

References

Aaker, J.L. 1997. "Dimensions of Brand Personality 1997." *Journal of Marketing Research* XXXIV, no. 3, pp. 347–356. doi:10.2307/3151897.

Aaker, J., K.D. Vohs, and C. Mogilner. 2010. "Nonprofits Are Seen as Warm and For-Profits as Competent: Firm Stereotypes Matter." *Journal of Consumer Research* 37, no. 2, pp. 224–237. doi:10.1086/651566.

American Red Cross. 2021. "Mission & Values." Retrieved from www.redcross.org/about-us/who-we-are/mission-and-values.

Anand, S. n.d. "Importance of Social Media Marketing in the Post-COVID-19 Era." Retrieved from www.socialpilot.co/blog/social-media-marketing-in-post-covid-19-era (accessed August 17, 2021).

Burgess, C. and M. Burgess. 2014. *The Social Employee*. New York, NY: Mc-Graw Hill.

Chen, J. August 2020. "Brand Voice: What It Is & Why It Matters." https://sproutsocial.com/insights/brand-voice/.

Dillerm, C. 2015. "CodeCrush 2015: IT Innovation." Retrieved from http://slideplayer.com/slide/5788528/.

Effing, R. and T.A.M. Spil. 2016. "The Social Strategy Cone: Towards a Framework for Evaluating Social Media Strategies." *International Journal of Information Management* 36, no. 1, pp. 1–8. doi:10.1016/j.ijinfomgt.2015.07.009.

Fontanella, C. 2020. *32 Social Media Stats That Customer Service Reps Should Know in 2020*. https://blog.hubspot.com/service/social-media-stats.

Global HR Research. 2015. "The Pros and Cons of Social Media Screening." Retrieved from www.ghrr.com/blog/2015/11/13/the-pros-and-cons-of-social-media-screening/.

Gorbatch, A. May 10, 2019. "4 Inspiring Social Listening Examples From Brands Doing It Right." www.jeffbullas.com/social-listening-examples/.

Grieve, P. May 12, 2021. "Millennials vs. Gen Z: How Their Customer Service Expectations Compare." www.zendesk.com/blog/millennials-vs-gen-z-customer-service-expectations-compare/.

Kane, G.C. 2014. "Why Social Media Will Fundamentally Change Business." *MIT Sloan Management Review*. https://sloanreview.mit.edu/article/why-social-media-will-fundamentally-change-business/.

Katona, Z. and M. Sarvary. 2014. "Maersk Line: B2B Social Media—'It's Communication, Not Marketing.'" *California Management Review* 56, no. 3, pp. 142–156. doi:10.1525/cmr.2014.56.3.142.

Kiron, D. 2012. "SAP: Using Social Media for Building, Selling and Supporting." *MIT Sloan Management Review* 54, no. 1, pp. 1–4. Retrieved from http://sloanreview.mit.edu/feature/sap-using-social-media-for-building-selling-and-supporting/.

Li, C. and B. Solis. 2013. "The Evolution of Social Business: Six Stages of Social Media Transformation." www.slideshare.net/Altimeter/the-evolution-of-social-business-six-stages-of-social-media-transformation.

McKinsey & Company. 2020. "How COVID-19 Has Pushed Companies Over the Technology Tipping Point—and Transformed Business Forever." Retrieved from www.mckinsey.com/business-functions/strategy-and-corporate-finance/our-insights/how-covid-19-has-pushed-companies-over-the-technology-tipping-point-and-transformed-business-forever (accessed August 17, 2021).

Moreno, L. 2020. "6 of the Best B2B Brands on Social Media Now—Social Media Strategies Summit Blog." *Social Media Strategies Summit*. https://blog.socialmediastrategiessummit.com/top-b2b-brands-on-social-media/.

Morrison, C. January 14, 2021. "9 B2B Social Media Examples to Inspire Your Strategy." https://everyonesocial.com/blog/b2b-social-media-examples/.

Newberry, C. January 12, 2021. "38 LinkedIn Statistics Marketers Should Know in 2021." https://blog.hootsuite.com/linkedin-statistics-business/.

Novell. 2013. "Enterprise Technology Through the Years." Retrieved from https://infostory.com/2013/09/15/timeline-of-enterprise-technology/.

Pew Research Center. April 07, 2021. "Demographics of Social Media Users and Adoption in the United States." www.pewresearch.org/internet/fact-sheet/social-media/.

Pfeffer, J., T. Zorbach, and K.M. Carley. 2014. "Understanding Online Firestorms: Negative Word-of-Mouth Dynamics in Social Media Networks." *Journal of Marketing Communications* 20, no. 1–2, pp. 117–128. doi:10.1080/13527266.2013.797778.

Polt, R. 1995. "A Brief History of Typewriters." *The Classic Typewriter Page*. http://site.xavier.edu/polt/typewriters/tw-history.html.

PR Newswire. January 21, 2021. "Future of Recruiting Study Finds 76 Percent of Employers Predict Hiring Demand Will Near or Surpass Pre-Pandemic Levels in 2021." www.prnewswire.com/news-releases/future-of-recruiting-study-finds-76-percent-of-employers-predict-hiring-demand-will-near-or-surpass-pre-pandemic-levels-in-2021-301212295.html.

PR Web. October 14, 2020. "71% of Hiring Decision-Makers Agree Social Media Is Effective for Screening Applicants." www.prweb.com/releases/71_of_hiring_decision_makers_agree_social_media_is_effective_for_screening_applicants/prweb17467312.htm.

Sagefrog Marketing Group. 2021. "2021 B2B Marketing Mix Report Top Takeaways." www.sagefrog.com/blog/2021-b2b-marketing-mix-report-top-takeaways/.

SAP. 2015. "2015 Annual Report." Retrieved from http://go.sap.com/docs/download/investors/2015/sap-2015-annual-report.pdf.

SAP. 2016. "Company Information." http://go.sap.com/corporate/en/company.fast-facts.html.

Statista. 2020. "Social Media Average Daily Usage by U.S. Users 2022." www.statista.com/statistics/1018324/us-users-daily-social-media-minutes/.

Statista. 2021. "Social Media Platforms Used by B2B & B2C Marketers 2021." www.statista.com/statistics/259382/social-media-platforms-used-by-b2b-and-b2c-marketers-worldwide/.

Stich, L., G. Golla, and A. Nanopoulos. 2014. "Modelling the Spread of Negative Word-of-Mouth in Online Social Networks." *Journal of Decision Systems* 23, no. 2. pp. 203–221. doi:10.1080/12460125.2014.886494.

van Luxemburg, A. 2011. "Social Media Maturity Model." Retrieved from www.slideshare.net/AntoonvanL/social-media-maturity-model.

Williams, T. 2012. "The Evolution of Technology & Its Impact on the Development of Social Businesses." *Forbes*. Retrieved from https://visual.ly/community/Infographics/technology/evolution-technology-its-impact-development-social-businesses.

CHAPTER 4

Storytelling

No one is going to share your message if it is not worth sharing. Not a novel idea—yet, marketers are spending a considerable amount of time thinking about the types of information or content they should post online. There is now recognition that the old outbound model of marketing—where marketers seek out consumers via cold calls and unsolicited advertisements—is not working. Consumers need to come to you (i.e., inbound marketing). However, you need something of substance to lure them in; good content embedded in a larger brand story. You also need to be a darn good storyteller.

This focus on delivering valuable content underlines the growing area of content marketing. Content marketing is defined by the Content Marketing Institute as "a strategic marketing approach focused on creating and distributing valuable, relevant, and consistent content to attract and retain a clearly-defined audience—and, ultimately, to drive profitable customer action" (Content Marketing Institute n.d.). Since 2011, interest in content marketing has steadily grown (Snow 2015). A cottage industry has been developed resulting in numerous dedicated software platforms designed to help you create, curate, optimize, analyze, and distribute digital assets (Lieb, Groopman, and Li 2014). In addition, there are also content-marketing conferences and the Content Marketing Institute dedicated to the topic. Content marketing is essential because it is not only the backbone of social media marketing but also search engine optimization (SEO) practices, inbound marketing, and e-mail marketing. Success is measured by web traffic, search engine rankings, brand awareness, lead generations, sale revenue, downloads, and engagement such as social media.

The Content Marketing Institute definition provides a procedural overview of content marketing, yet it misses the mark somewhat, in that, it neglects the heart and soul of content marketing—storytelling.

For this, we turn to the content marketing tech agency Contently who defines content marketing as "the use of storytelling to build relationships with consumers by providing them something entertaining or useful" (Contently 2016). In truth, storytelling is only a part of the message communication process. In an analysis of blogs, researchers Kozinets et al. (2010) found that word-of-mouth marketing (WOMM) was influenced by "character narratives" (i.e., personal stories), the specific forum or message context, communal norms found within the forum (i.e., norms impacting communication message "expression, transmission, and reception"), and the marketing message and meaning (i.e., marketing promotional elements) (Kozinets et al. 2010). This chapter will explore each of these WOMM influences within the context of brand story development, message development, textual storytelling, and visual storytelling process. The chapter concludes with how to write a more persuasive story that will ultimately drive consumer action.

What Is Your Brand Story?

Storytelling is central to this chapter because WOMM is about *sharing* stories—stories that engage and excite consumers; stories that consumers consider valuable. Understanding the social consumer, their interests and passions, and preferences when it comes to media consumption is at the core of spinning a good, authentic tale. Social media brings with it a whole set of storytelling tools—the written word, pictures, video, and even virtual reality are all at our disposal. Social media also provides brands with easy ways to retell stories by allowing retweeting, sharing, and embedding to be so accessible.

Marketers who want to excel in social word of mouth (sWOM) marketing must think of themselves as storytellers and consumers not just as their audience but also as their coauthors. And, like any good storyteller, they need to tailor their story and manner of delivery for their audience. Marketers need to be able to both identify and cultivate storytellers from the consumer rank and acknowledge that they are "coproducers" of marketing communications (Kozinets et al. 2010). Consumers should be encouraged to share their experiences, and marketers should routinely select and profile key stories that are consistent with the overall brand narrative. In the end, the focus needs to be on *telling before selling*. So, how do you capture a consumer's attention for them to not only view but share your content? What story will you share? How is your story going to be different from your competitors?

There are numerous examples of companies and individuals who have successfully embraced storytelling in their marketing efforts. Arguably, one of the best-known examples of applying storytelling in their marketing efforts is Red Bull. In fact, Red Bull's marketing is so interwoven with content development that it can be thought of as a "publishing empire that also happens to sell a beverage" (O'Brien 2012). Red Bull's content covers a variety of extreme sports and documents their sponsored events, individual athletes, and teams through a variety of social media platforms. All of these efforts are consistent with their lifestyle brand narrative of extreme action and sports. Red Bull further reinforces their story focus through the web series "Red Bull Storyteller." These stories move away from extreme sports athletes and instead highlight "everyday" consumers encountering extreme situations (i.e., illness, ecology threats, NYC street hustle).

Another example of a company putting brand stories at the center of its marketing efforts is the Coca-Cola Company. In 2011, Coca-Cola began to focus on "content excellence." The underlying theme of which was to create "contagious ideas" communicated through dynamic brand stories that would drive conversation online. Coca-Cola even changed its company website from a corporate presence to one more along the lines of a digital magazine—called "Coca-Cola Journey" (Elliot 2012). Coca-Cola's overriding brand story is helping the world live positively. Ten years later, in 2021, Coca-Cola adjusted its story to embrace a new brand philosophy—Real Magic (Coca-Cola 2021a). Real magic is "when we come together in unexpected moments that elevate the everyday into the extraordinary" (Courie 2021). During the 2021 Christmas season, Coca-Cola spread this "real magic" by randomly sending customers a video via Cameo of the iconic Coca-Cola Santa video. They also allowed customers to sign up for personalized Santa messages that could notably be shared on social media (Coca-Cola 2021b). Lastly, TOMS shoes present a story about improving lives. Shifting away from its buy one, give one away model, TOMS now donates one-third of its profits. Specifically, they now provide grants to organizations that focus on supporting mental health, "increasing access to opportunities," and preventing gun violence (Toms 2022).

So, Red Bull's story is about extreme action infused with energy, Coca-Cola wants to bring to the world real magic, TOMS is improving lives—but what is your big brand story? The rules of writing and communicating your brand story are very similar to those contained in your local public library. You need good, relatable characters, an interesting and compelling story reinforced by supporting content, and a descriptive and effective way to executive it (Content Marketing Institute n.d.; Gunelius 2013). Social media, thankfully, has provided us with numerous platforms that make this process easier.

Keys to Successful Storytelling

There are six keys to successful storytelling: character, brand voice, "big" story brand idea, story arc, story execution, and coauthorship.

Later, in this chapter, we will discuss many strategies to help your message's virality—but at a minimum, it is about good storytelling.

- **Character:** Whether it is an influencer, employee, or a profiled consumer, characters that convey your brand's content should be someone that your buyer persona can relate to and finds credible. They can play a leading or supporting role in your story, but your consumer needs to develop an emotional connection with your character(s). Therefore, ensuring the message is ripe with information for character development (i.e., video or images) will increase the likelihood that the consumer will not only be engaged but also share the message.
- **Brand voice:** The voice of your brand—conveyed through text and visually oriented posts—must be consistent; consistent between posts and consistent with the brand image and story. Are the brand voice and subsequent language used informal or formal? Is the personality conveyed—fun,

sarcastic, witty, stoic, and so on? Can consumers quickly pick up on personality characteristics (i.e., Intel's voice is smart and enlightening; Taco Bell is a little wacky)? As we discussed in Chapter 3, it takes a lot of work to establish, achieve, and maintain a consistent brand voice.

- **"Big" brand story idea:** The story should be simple and get at the core of your brand's identity. It may seek to explain why your company exists or delve into a problem that your product seeks to resolve. Ultimately, the big brand story must be appealing to your consumers—it must emotionally connect with them. It is hard to think of a more compelling brand story than TOMS shoes. Look to your company's mission to help develop your brand story.
- **Story arc:** Brand stories are a collection of information or posts—not told in one sitting. However, posts must be consistent with the larger brand story. Also, like any good story, there should be hurdles and ways to overcome them delivered in regularly scheduled increments. The presented conflict should be something that relates to your consumer's needs and stage in the purchasing cycle. A great example of a compelling story can be found in Red Bull's Instagram highlights of Eileen Gui's 2022 Olympic wins and experience.
- **Story execution:** Social media is the instrument of story delivery and also provides a framework for the types and methodology of how the stories are told. Stories can be short (e.g., TikTok) or complex (e.g., YouTube channel). They can also be told across multiple social media platforms. The key to selecting where to execute your story is both understanding which social media platforms your consumers are using and knowing the type of content or story they want and expect to be told within a specific network. For example, the content on Pinterest tends to be more "home-orientated" (i.e., food and so on) (Moon 2014; Libert 2014).

(Continues)

- **Coauthorship (with consumers):** Lastly, it is essential to remember that brand stories are not just the product of orchestrated marketing campaigns born out of corporate boardrooms—they are cocreated with consumers. Consumers are routinely sharing their brand stories, and experiences with the product. Messages on social media related to products are stories—tales of consumers' experiences and connections with the product that are positive, negative, and neutral. Brands must nurture and encourage their consumers to tell their stories.

Story Content and Making It Contagious

So, how will you tell your story on social media? As mentioned, your individual posts must reinforce your brand story, but above all, they must be interesting and valuable to consumers. This is especially true if you want consumers to share your story. However, simply getting a consumer to view or read your post does not guarantee its virality. Let's face it; the vast majority of posted content within social media is simply not shared with others. In fact, most fans of branded pages do not even see the Facebook posts in their newsfeed, let alone "like" or "share" them. So, what should you do? The answer to not only getting exposure on platforms like Facebook but also getting users to share, retweet, and repin comes down to one simple truth: you must provide content that *your* consumers value.

Value, much like beauty, is in the eye of the beholder. And, it will also vary from consumer group to consumer group. Fortunately, research examining virality and word-of-mouth (WOM) communication provides us with some tools to increase the likelihood of creating shareable content. Jonah Berger, Wharton Professor and author of *Contagious*, identified six principles (STEPPS) that drive WOM: Social Currency, Triggers, Emotion, Public, Practical Value, and Stories (Berger 2013). We will briefly explore each of these principles as they relate to social media content. We have chosen to vary the order provided in his STEPPS acronym and discuss emotion last—given its importance in the academic literature.

- **Social currency**: We care deeply concerned how we appear to other people. And, social media affords us the ability to craft, in some cases, a new and improved digital identity. Consumers, therefore, seek out and share interesting information that is consistent with their desired self. They want to stand out and look good in the eyes of their peers. This can also explain the sharing success of social media posts that include "quotes" (Zarrella 2013b). As a marketer, you need to think about the types of information that consumers will want to share to look "good" and also how to put a spotlight on consumers. This may mean rewarding or simply acknowledging consumers who actively post their product reviews or get the most views on social media. You can also give certain consumers the "inside track" on new product-related information. At a minimum, you should highlight what makes your product or rather your product benefits interesting to consumers.
- **Triggers**: The secret behind triggers is getting your content to be "top-of-mind." In other words, people will readily be prompted to think about the content (and then share it). Use specific events (i.e., holidays or big news events), activities (i.e., vacation time), or obstacles (i.e., the morning rush out the door with your children) that your target consumer encounters and align them with your content. Think—Star Wars "may the force be with you" aligned with May 4 "May the fourth be with you." Also, make sure you time messages to when these events and obstacles occur.
- **Public**: Make something stand out so that people can identify it and imitate it. While this suggestion was made about creating a highly visible product (i.e., silver-colored Apple computers that contain a backlit apple versus the typical black laptops), it is also relevant in the context of social media. To illustrate, make your content more visible by simply creating a post that contains a photo, video, animated GIF, or cinemagraph. Increasing its visibility allows it to be more easily noticed and shared (more on this later). You can also create a branded sound that begins or ends each of your videos. Think

about the very beginning of TED talk videos—the distinctive sound of chimes, a water drop, and then drums (can you hear it?). Another idea is to always include identifiers on your branded content to quickly and readily assign its ownership to you. This can be easily accomplished by putting a small logo at the corner of a post or video.

- **Practical value**: Many of us simply enjoy useful information and want to spread its value to others. It should come as no surprise that some of the most valuable content is, in fact, instructive and educational posts. Leading Marketing Solution Providers 2015, for example, an analysis of BuzzSumo (they keep track of popular social media posts) articles found that longer posts (2000+ words) are shared more often than shorter posts. Furthermore, infographics and lists outperformed videos when it came to sharing (Kagan 2017). When analyzing retweets, Quicksprout found that tweets linked to "how-to" and "list-based" articles performed well with retweets (Quicksprout 2021). So, the question is—What does your target consumer consider valuable and how can you simply convey this information? Lists, videos, infographics, how-to guides, and frequently asked questions are a good place to start.

- **Stories**: Up to this point, we have discussed the broad brand story, but within this larger context, there are smaller stories, individual consumer, or employee stories that work to support the bigger story theme. Take, for example, the storied posts on Redbull's dedicated racing Instagram page. Within it, numerous posts highlight Formula 1 Racing 2021 World Champion Max Verstappen. In fact, they even have a dedicated story highlight reel that celebrates his win, the reaction from his support crew, and fan reaction watching in the Netherlands (where he is from).

- **Emotions**: Content that conveys emotion readily goes viral. Yet, all emotions are not created equally. Emotions that are high in arousal (e.g., anger and awe) tend to have higher rates of sharing. Whereas, low-arousal emotions (e.g., sadness) do not inspire as much sharing—no one wants to feel or responsible for making others feel miserable. Research suggests that just having a more emotional headline for your content can lead to a higher share rate (Moon 2014). There is a free analyzer tool, the emotional marketing value headline analyzer, that will rate the emotional impact of your headline (Advanced Marketing Institute 2009). A message's overall associated emotion and the general valence of a message—positive, negative, and neutral—have garnered a lot of research in the academic literature. As such, we provide further elaboration of both message valence and emotional arousal in the next section.

Message Valence and Emotional Arousal

Academics and industry frequently look at WOM messages from a valence or sentiment perspective. In other words, is the information or comment positive, negative, or neutral? While marketers can certainly communicate positive, negative, or neutral information, most often discussions about sentiment relate more to product-related consumer comments and reactions and their consequences. Traditional WOM research has found negative WOM to be more influential on both brand evaluations and on purchase intentions (Bone 1995; Richins 1983; Brown and Reingen 1987). The same has been found for eWOM communications—negative eWOM significantly impacts experiential and more sensory-dependent type goods (Park and Lee 2009). For better or worse, social media allows for the rapid diffusion of negative sWOM information. This dissemination of negative information within social media differs from other WOM and eWOM in its speed and volume, ability to weigh into the conversation in simplistic terms ("like" or retweet), the "echo chamber" of social media (i.e., when consumers are not exposed to new ideas within your network, instead existing ideas are amplified through repetitive postings), the amount of information, and cross-media dynamics (i.e., blurring of online and offline media) (Pfeffer, Zorbach, and Carley 2014). Negative sWOM can be particularly detrimental if it originates with key social influencers such as "hubs" and "bridges" (Stich, Golla, and Nanopoulos 2014). This can be incredibly harmful to a business ("Pink Slime Case Study").

> Texas mom Bettina Elias Siegel ignited a social media firestorm that destroyed a business. Siegel was on a mission to improve the quality of school lunches. She was concerned with the widespread use of a product known as Lean Finely Textured Beef (LFTB)—lean beef that has been extracted from the fat trimmings, a staple of the fast-food industry commonly found in burgers, tacos, and school lunches. Whereas the name LFTB sounds harmless enough, the product because of its color and texture acquired the unappetizing moniker, "Pink Slim." Siegel turned to her blog, The Lunch Tray, to express her disgust and outrage, calling on lawmakers to ban the product from the federal school lunch program. Within eight days of her posting, more than 200,000 concerned parents had signed an online petition. Siegel's beef (pun intended) spreads like wildfire and was picked up by ABC news. In response, supermarkets abandoned the product, and fast-food chains, such as Wendy's, felt the need to reassure consumers—Wendy's took out a series of newspaper advertisements to assure consumers that they have never used the product. Beef Products Inc. (BPI), the producer of "Pink Slime," suffered irreversible financial losses and was forced to suspend operations in three of its four plants. AFA Foods, a meat processing company, declared bankruptcy and U.S. sales of ground beef hit a ten-year low. (ElBoghdady 2012)

Negative posts can also be incredibly harmful to social systems—such as politics. An analysis was conducted of approximately 2.7 million Facebook posts and Twitter tweets drawn for the accounts of politicians and media outlets from the United States. The study found that posts criticizing or mocking the "political outgroup" (i.e., opposing party) were shared twice as many times as positive posts from their own party. These findings also extended to emojis (i.e., more "angry face emojis" on political rival posts versus "heart-shaped" emojis on favored candidates). No effect differences were found between Facebook and Twitter (Lewsey n.d.)

Industry and academic research reveal that there are differences in how users of various social media platforms respond to positive, negative, or neutral sentiments. In a study using simulated Pinterest boards, consumers paid more attention to negative sWOM than positive or neutral (Daugherty and Hoffman 2014). An analysis of Facebook posts revealed that neutral posts received fewer likes than positive or negative posts, whereas very negative posts received more comments (Murphy 2012). Finally, Buzzsumo and Fractl conducted an industry study that examined the sharing of one million articles across five different social media platforms and found that some users on platforms had sentiment preferences. Specifically, users on LinkedIn and Pinterest tended to share more positive stories, whereas Facebook shared the most negative among the five platforms reviewed. Twitter and Google+ had the "most balanced range of sentiments" (Libert 2014).

Should we simply view social media posts as positive, negative, or neutral? What about specific emotions and their strength? What role do they play in virality? The strength of the emotion—or emotional arousal—is what leads people to take action or share the message. To be more specific, high emotional arousal content that generates awe, excitement, or humor performs well. In addition, even negative high-arousal emotions such as anger or anxiety are very shareable (Berger 2013). However, emotions that do not elicit high arousal, such as general sadness and contentment, are not viral. An examination of the most frequently e-mailed *New York Times* articles found that articles that instilled a sense of awe defined as "emotion of self-transcendence, a feeling of admiration and elevation the face of something greater than the self" performed the best (Tierney 2010). Positive content was shared more often than negative content (Berger and Milkman 2011). These findings were reinforced in a separate study that looked at viral videos—high-arousal, positive valence specifically those that inspired the emotion of exhilaration—were shared the most frequently (Nelson-Field, Riebe, and Sharp 2013). In contrast, a study that addressed emoticons use within the Chinese social media platform Weibo found that rage was more viral than joy, sadness, or disgust (Shaer 2014). While the studies contained different conclusions, the importance of high-arousal emotions in sharing remained the same. Furthermore, it may be wise to stay away from negative high-arousal emotions as we do not yet understand the long-term effects it would have on a brand (Nelson-Field, Riebe, and Sharp 2013).

The problem for companies is, of course, how do you create content that arouses our sense of awe, humor, anger, excitement, or anxiety enough to get shared? The answer lies at least, in part, in selecting an appropriate creative strategy.

Creative Strategies

Creative strategies can be thought of as "executional factors and message strategies used to bridge the gap between what the marketer wants to say and what the consumer needs to hear" (Ashley and Tuten 2015, 18). Some different typologies of traditional media have been developed (Laskey, Day, and Crask 1989; Aaker and Norris 1982). But, how do they relate to social media? In a review of the social media content posted on 28 popular consumer brands across multiple social media platforms, researchers Ashley and Tuten (2015) identified the most popular message strategies (see Figure 4.1 for an overview). They found a variety of creative strategies were being used; the most popular of which was a functional appeal. A functional appeal demonstrates the utility of a product. Despite

✓ Message Strategies

1. Functional appeal
Focus on the functionality or utility of a product or service.

7. Exclusivity
Emphasize that the product or service is only for a select few. limited quantity, time, place, etc.

2. Resonance
Repetition of elements such as congruence between images and words.

8. Animation
Add motion to static images.

3. Experiential appeal
Highlight the services (sight, sound, taste, touch, smell).

8. Comparative
Directly or indirectly compare your product or service against the competition.

4. Emotional appeal
Emphasize how a product or service will make you feel.

10. Spokesperson
Include a person to speak on behalf of the company.

5. Unique selling proposition
Highlight what makes you different from the competition.

11. Spokescharacter
Create a fictional character to speak on behalf of the company (e.g., cartoon character).

6. Social cause
Associate your company with a social cause.

Figure 4.1 Creative message strategies

its popular use, functional appeal approaches were not related to the levels of engagement, social influence, or the number of Facebook fans or Twitter followers.

Ashley and Tuten (2015) also found that brands attempted to engage with consumers by inviting them to share some content, and half of the brands studied encouraged sharing by providing incentives. The results found that there was a significant relationship between the incentive to share content and the number of people following a brand, Facebook fans, social influence score (i.e., Klout), and engagement scores. Contests that offered consumers the chance to win a prize were twice as popular as discounts (Ashley and Tuten 2015). Outside of identifying a variety of appeals and illustrating which appeals are more successful in driving consumer action, these findings highlight an important truth: Do not focus on selling within social media. As the poor performance on the functional appeal illustrates, content posted on social media cannot be solely about your product. Instead, engage with your consumers, provide value, and focus on appeals that include text and images, and emotion, which engages the senses and associates your company with a cause.

Textual Storytelling

Now that you have figured out your brand story and the general content of your story, you need to decide how to execute it. For better or worse, you need to adjust your writing style to conform to the ever-evolving social media lexicon and technology platforms. There are also some other considerations that you need to make if you want to increase the likelihood of your posts being shared.

Length

If you want to increase shareability, in some cases, shorter is better. For example, Buzzsumo found that Facebook posts with 0 to 50 characters had, on average, the highest levels of engagement (Hutchinson 2019). While you can post a long Instagram caption (up to 2,200 characters), the platform truncates them to 125 characters. Like Facebook, posts with 50 characters or less receive more interactions (Quintly 2019). See a trend?

Twitter, however, proves to be the exception. In 2017, Twitter increased its character count limit to 280. Longer tweets in this "expanded range" typically see higher levels of engagement (Gessler 2020).

Acronyms

Acronyms—immigrants from texting language—have become an integral part of the social space. Marketers have a vast number of acronyms at their disposal, and they can be an effective and fun way to communicate with your consumers (Figure 4.2). There are also commonly used Acronyms used in B2B social media communications (e.g., CPC—Cost per Click; CTA—Call to Action; SMB—Small- and Mid-Size/Medium

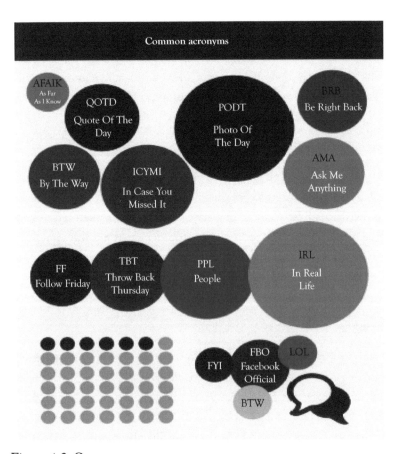

Figure 4.2 Common acronyms

Businesses) (Zote 2020). While most of the acronyms are familiar and self-explanatory (e.g., OMG, LOL, DM), some are a little more complicated. Take, for instance, BAE (Before Anyone Else), which can mean a close friend, or a person's spouse, girlfriend, partner, or FBO (Facebook Official), which marks a life event change that you are making public.

Before you jump on the acronym bandwagon, you need to understand whether using particular acronyms is consistent with your brand voice, and are these acronyms used by your target market. Chances are your target market actively uses only a small number of the acronyms, or they have developed new terms unique to their cohort. According to Askfm (a popular youth-driven social networking site), teens readily use a host of novel acronyms to capture their zeitgeist (TBR = to be rude; SMH = shaking my head; IDEK = I don't even know; OOTD = outfit of the day) (Askfm 2022). There is some evidence that using an acronym can make your social media post less sharable. This has been found to be true with "LOL" (Zarrella 2009). And, when comparing the use of RT versus actually spelling out "retweet" or "please retweet," the full-length version comes out on top.

Word Choice

It is not just what you say, but how you say it! Word choice and phrases can dramatically impact whether a post is shared.

Strong copy (and the interesting ideas behind them) is mandatory. This means that word choice needs to follow the 4Cs of copywriting: clear, concise, compelling, and credible (Bly 2013). Writing to be understood by your target market is a given. This means that you need to select words at the vocabulary level of your intended audience (e.g., no advanced GRE/LSAT words for most folks) and be to the point. As a general rule, select your words carefully, avoid rambling, and if appropriate, list items (with or without emojis). Be interesting when you write and make it relevant and entertaining to your reader. Consumers need to feel like they are authentically communicating with the brand. In other words, are the words consistent with the brand voice?

Outside of general word-related guidance, copywriting gurus also rely on what is referred to as "power words." Power words provoke a psychological response because both persuasive and can trigger an emotional response. Ultimately, they can nudge people to take action. In truth, the power word list is long (just Google it); however, here is a small selection organized by emotion: *Greed Power Words*: Bargain, Discount, Exclusive, Frugal, Limited, Reduced, Save, Ultimate; *Curiosity Power Words*: Astonishing, Be the first, Classified, Limited, Stunning, Top Secret, Unexplained; *Sloth Power Words*: All-inclusive, Complete, Freebie, Instant, Minutes, Painless, Steal, Template; *Lust Power Words*: Captivating, Desire, Exotic, Mind-blowing, Obsession, Sinful, Thrilling, Wild; *Vanity Power Words*: Amazing, Beautiful, Brilliant, Epic, Genius, Hero, Smart, Ultimate; *Trust Power Words*: Authentic, Best-selling, Certified, Expert, Guaranteed, Official, Reliable, Verify; *Anger Power Words*: Abuse, Bullshit, Evil, Greedy, Punish, Sneaky, Victim, Worst; *Fear Power Words*: Assault, Beware, Danger, Embarrass, Horrific, Mistake, Panic, Terror (Fernandez 2020).

Influential writing is important, yet what gets shared? In an effort to better understand what headlines receive the most engagement, BuzzSumo analyzed 100 million articles in 2020 (Linehan, Rayson, and Chiu 2021). Their analysis revealed "trigrams"—popular three-word phrases that had the highest levels of engagement on Facebook. These phrases could be found at the start, middle, or end of a headline. Following are the top 10 Facebook headline trigram phrases:

1. of the year
2. in X years
3. for the first
4. the first time
5. one of the
6. you need to
7. need to know
8. X years in
9. on social media
10. to know about

The most engaged headlines shared information related to ranking (e.g., the person of the year), newness (e.g., for the first time in 20 years), hyperbole, instructional (i.e., crucial information), surprise (e.g., shocking fact), curiosity (e.g., only 20 percent of people got X correct, can you?), guidance (e.g., how to), and story (i.e., case study). Overall, the most frequently used theme on Facebook was instructional. If people believed the information was "need to know," they were more likely to engage and share it. BuzzSumo also analyzed the beginning of Facebook headlines. This analysis revealed the popularity of "listicles" that centered primarily on providing guidance through "how-tos." So, while not very sexy, the most common word used for highly engaged headlines was "The" followed by "New," "A," "How," and "This." BuzzSumo replicated their analysis on Twitter and found similar results across the platforms with some exceptions; curiosity and story-related headlines significantly performed better on Twitter. In conclusion, if you want to write a headline that is likely to be shared on both Facebook and Twitter, your best bet is one of these top 10 phrases (Linehan, Rayson, and Chiu 2021):

1. the story of
2. the top X
3. the X best
4. the X most
5. this is how
6. this is the
7. what are the
8. what is the
9. what you need
10. why you should

Call-to-Action (CTA)

Marketers must also ask for what they want. If you want a retweet, ask for a retweet. If you want a like, ask, share, then ask, follow, ask, reply, ask, download, ask (you get the idea). The adage—ask, and you will receive is alive and well on social media. However, that is not to say that every social post should include a CTA—you do not want to come across as needy or pushy. CTAs should be incentivized by posting good content or creating a contest (Romanek 2013). You also should utilize action-oriented words and if relevant power words. And it doesn't hurt to add a little urgency (e.g., time is running out, call today!). That said, some CTAs work better than others. Following is a list from highest to lowest of the top seven words or phrases that when included in a tweet garnered more retweets than did similar tweets that did not contain these words (Zarrella 2013a). As you can see, having good manners pays off.

- Please Help
- Please Retweet
- Please RT
- Please
- Retweet
- Spread
- Visit

While the preceding list pertains to Twitter, Facebook posts containing CTA words such as "like," "comment," and "share" also result in higher levels of compliance than posts that did not integrate these words (Zarrella 2012). Similar results with CTA words were also found on Instagram and Pinterest (Ripen Ecommerce 2014; Zarrella 2014). Specifically, Instagram captions that included CTA words asking to "like" and "comment" had higher levels of engagement (Zarrella 2014). On Pinterest, "Please Repin" and "Please Like" should also drive action. The lesson here is that when you include a CTA, remember to say please.

Links One of the big benefits of social media for marketers is that social can drive traffic outside of the platform through the use of URL links and linked images. Not only do links offer the potential to drive up advertising revenue and conversion rates, but they also provide increased value to consumers by supplementing the information that can be contained in a short post. This increased value is apparent in that consumers are much more likely to retweet and share information from posts that include a link. To illustrate, one study found that retweeting was 86 percent higher with texts that included links (Patel 2014). Beyond providing links, specific content publishers may be more likely to produce engaging content. In particular, youtube.com, cnn.com, guardian.com, nytimes.com, and the washingtonpost.com had the most engaging

2019 and 2020 Twitter headlines, and youtube.com, rollingstone.com, cnn.com, dailymail.co.uk, and boredpanda.com had the most engaging 2019 and 2020 Facebook headlines (Linehan, Rayson, and Chiu 2021).

Hashtags The history of hashtags began in the late 1990s as a way to group items together on Internet Relay Chat. Designer and now-Uber employee Chris Messina co-opted their use to organize group conversation on Twitter in a tweet on August 23, 2007. Three years later, in 2010, Twitter reinforced their usage by emphasizing hashtags through "trending" topics on their front page (Bennett 2014a)—today they are ubiquitous. Users of Facebook, TikTok, Twitter, Instagram, Pinterest, and more use hashtags to organize subjects and photos as well as express their opinion or support on a topic. Hashtags have even entered everyday face-to-face conversational vernacular.

Not surprisingly, hashtags impact sharing. Industry research has found that using hashtags matters when it comes to retweets. Twitter's analysis of over two million tweets reported that hashtag use resulted in a 16 percent increase in retweets (Rogers 2014). Dan Zarrella's research found an even higher retweet rate—tweets that contained a hashtag were 55 percent more likely to be retweeted than tweets that did not use hashtags—#Amazing (Zarrella 2013b). However (and as we will discuss in Chapter 7), too many hashtags can be problematic and may present legal problems if they engulf disclosures. On Twitter, hashtags should be limited to no more than two particularly if you want to leave room for retweeting comments and substance. Two also seems to be the magic number on Facebook. However, Instagram and TikTok lend themselves to incorporating more hashtags in their search or discover features. Ayres 2015 Hashtags can either be location-based (e.g., place, city), branded (i.e., brand name, a specific campaign, or event), industry (i.e., marketing), community (i.e., #recoverytok), and descriptive (i.e., #5k) (Warren 2021).

One of the reasons that hashtags successfully impact sharing is that consumers can quickly find relevant content by searching within a specific social media platform or via Google. Similar to SEO practices, it is essential to create or identify meaningful hashtags that your consumers can relate to and that are relevant to your product. When creating hashtags, make sure they are unique to your brand, easy to remember, and relatively short. Also, make sure that there is no secondary meaning or the chance that consumers could misread and, therefore, misinterpret your intended hashtag meaning (e.g., The 2009 Britain's Got Talent Susan's Boyle PR team uses #susanalbumparty to announce the album release party—do you see the problem?). When you participate in an ongoing hashtag conversation, know what you are jumping into. Many marketers have not fully understood the meaning behind the hashtag conversation or were ignorant of the larger cultural context a trending topic was meant to illustrate and have quickly regretted their participation. Take, for instance, the dessert company Entenmann's who tweeted about not feeling bad or #NotGuilty about eating some of their low-calorie options. Unfortunately, #Not Guilty was currently being used to discuss the Casey Anthony trial verdict (Guido 2016). To assist you in finding the perfect hashtag, review hashtag use of competitors and social media influencers, keep track of trending hashtags on specific platforms and utilize a social media listening tool.

Quotes Quotes do well across social platforms. To illustrate, Twitter's analysis of over two million tweets found tweets that contained a quote received a retweet rate of 19 percent higher, whereas social media scientist, Dan Zarrella, found that tweeted quotes were more likely to be retweeted by 30 percent (Zarrella 2013b; Rogers 2014). Another analysis of approximately 400,000 tweets found that, and I quote, "users who tweeted quotes had 43% more followers" (QuickSprout 2021). While you have the option of including the quote with attribution in a tweet or on a Facebook post, a better approach is to overlay a quote over-an awe-inspiring photo for maximum effect. The power of visuals in social media cannot be overstated. Visual storytelling is an essential part of social media—as the next section will reveal.

Visual Storytelling: A Picture (or Video) Says a Thousand Words

Social media is increasingly becoming a visual medium. In 2021, it was predicted that 82 percent of all global Internet traffic will be from video (Cisco 2016). Visually oriented social media platforms such as Instagram, TikTok, and Snapchat have seen incredibly high adoption rates of growth. This observation coupled with the popularity of the "Stories" feature (short videos found at the top of platforms' feeds) makes it safe to assume that the majority of social media networking sites' data volume also revolves around visuals. The amount of visual data produced and shared on social media each day is truly staggering: 3.2 billion photos and 720,000 hours of video per day (Queensland University of Technology 2020). Smartphone adoption, continued advancements in digital camera technology, and a growing number of image- and video-centric social media platforms have led to a perfect storm of consumers wanting to use more images in their communications. This increasing reliance on visuals is consistent with research that has found that our visual IQ (as measured by Raven's Progressive Matrices nonverbal exam) is increasing faster than other aspects of our IQ (Kremer 2015). In 2015, the critical reading scores of high school graduates in the United States were the lowest they have been in 40 years. In the same year, writing scores, which they began testing in 2005, were the lowest on record (Kitroeff and Lorin 2015). The fact that our visual IQ is increasing and our reading and writing skills are decreasing highlights the importance of making your social posts rich with visual content.

Power of Images

The ability to get noticed within social media's ever-changing, information-rich environment is crucial. Consumers are experiencing information overload. E-mails, texts, and articles flood our screens. Photos, videos, and infographics assist consumers in their ability to digest data quickly. This is happening, in part, because by the time we reach 18 years of age, most of us will be visual learners. Simply put, many of us learn more through visual modalities: symbols, diagrams, pictures, and videos (Felder and Silberman 1988). Our brains also seem predisposed to visuals; approximately 30 percent of our cortex is dedicated to visual processing, whereas hearing only makes up 3 percent and touch is 8 percent (Grady 1993).

Research on traditional advertising and WOM has established that images are superior to text in garnering attention (Pieters and Wedel 2004; Singh et al. 2000). One study found that consumers are 90 percent more likely to look at an advertisement's primary picture before they look at the copy (Werner 1984). This could help explain why engagement is higher with social media posts that include images. There is, however, evidence to suggest that consumers may pay more attention to the text, as opposed to images when promoting luxury brands on social media. This may be attributed to the high level of perceived risk (e.g., monetary, social, and psychological risk) that consumers may associate with purchasing luxury items, resulting in a need for detailed information, which is typically contained in the text. Images were still more attention-grabbing for the nonluxury product (Hoffman and Daugherty 2013).

Images are also powerful because, as research suggests, we remember images (recall and recognition) more than we remember text (Childers and Houston 1984). This phenomenon has been called the picture superiority effect (Stenberg 2006; Paivio, Rogers, and Smythe 1968). This effect may not be unique to static images but also include videos. Research has shown that television commercials, more so than print ads, can influence purchase attitudes and intentions (Grass and Wallace 1974). More specifically, videos that evoke high-arousal emotions are remembered the most (Nelson-Field, Taylor, and Hartnett 2013). This relationship between high-arousal emotions and memory also highlights that one of the biggest benefits of images or videos is their ability to influence consumers' emotions. Images and video have the ability to quickly influence not only your consumers but also general public opinion. There have been numerous instances of a single photograph being credited for changing public sentiment (Pensiero 2015).

The Popularity of Visuals

The sheer volume of digital images captured and shared per day is astonishing. To illustrate, in every minute of the day (in 2021), TikTok users watch 167 million videos, Instagram users share 65,000 photos, YouTube users stream 694,000 hours, and two million Snapchats are sent (Domo 2021). The quick rise of visual-centric platforms (e.g., TikTok and Instagram), Facebook's Timeline redesign, which focuses more on images, the visibility of images and video included in tweets, and the integration of the "cover" photo and "Stories" across multiple platforms (i.e., Facebook, Twitter, and LinkedIn) all reinforce that we have entered "the age of visual culture" (Bullas 2012). Indeed, some marketers would argue that social media as a whole is shifting away from text and embracing the visual medium (Gupta 2013). The fact that the highest levels of engagement for millennials, as measured by average monthly minutes, occur on visual platforms (i.e., Facebook, Snapchat, and Instagram), suggests that this is the right strategy. Futurists predict that Generation Z (those born after 1996) will rely even more heavily on images to communicate than millennials (Meeker 2016). Smart brands need to make sure they are investing in visually-centric social media platforms. In particular, they should be on Instagram and TikTok, where brand engagement with consumers is higher than on Pinterest, Facebook, LinkedIn, and Twitter (Elliot 2015). TikTok actually has the highest (Cucu 2022).

Photos and Consumption Practices

Photos that are shared the most often do not typically contain pastoral images of the countryside, but rather they capture consumers' daily lives; lives that involve branded clothing, food, and activities and are contextualized within cars, stores, and restaurants. The ability to easily and quickly associate and communicate not only your opinion about a product but also your product aspirations, usage and ownership is incredibly powerful. In fact, certain types of visual platforms lend themselves to documenting specific points in the consumer decision-making and consumption process, with Pinterest and Instagram representing opposite ends of the consumption spectrum (Gupta 2013). Pinterest images that populate consumer boards are often taken from the brand's owned media (e.g., website) (Moore 2012). Pinterest boards become an aspirational, prepurchase wish list and work to drive sales to e-commerce websites. Ninety-three percent of users are using Pinterest in prepurchase planning (Shopify 2016), and the average order that originated from Pinterest is almost $59 (Bennett 2014b). In contrast, Instagram documents products that consumers own. It reflects their postpurchase use and conveys their satisfaction.

Photos that are posted on social media are often sanitized, filtered, and photoshopped versions. Uploaded photos are cherry-picked from a much larger set (Eveleth n.d.). Teens and adults alike are being careful in which digital artifacts they select to convey their desired digital identity. Part of presenting one's best self online is utilizing filters. Filters are used to correct perceived problems and improve aesthetics, and create unique fun photos. Highlighting specific objects in the photo, changing the color, and applying vintage effects are other motivations for using filters (Bakhshi et al. 2014). Not surprisingly, filters can impact engagement, although the results are somewhat mixed. A study analyzing 7.6 million Flickr photos found that filtered photos increased viewing by 21 percent and were likely to have attracted 45 percent more comments (Bakhshi et al. 2014). In contrast, an Instagram study found that photos with "no filter" applied generated the highest number of likes per follower (Zarrella 2014). While the novelty of some basic filters has worn off for consumers, augmented reality (AR) filters have a lot of potential to increase brand engagement and conversions. Want to see how a new shade of lipstick or sunglasses looks on you? Now you can. AR filters are immersive and offer consumers a fun brand experience.

Videos and Other Digital Assets

Videos are another increasingly important sWOM tool. This is especially true now that Instagram allows video posts to be between 3 seconds and 10 minutes, video platform TikTok's high engagement, and the "Stories" feature popularity. Increasingly, social media serves to capture consumer or brand micro-moments via video. Consumers seem to appreciate the increased media richness as seen through the soaring popularity of Instagram and TikTok. Videos also seem to capture spontaneous and authentic moments. And these "real" moments are arguably best illustrated through the temporary, 24-hour "Stories" feature. While Snapchat birthed the feature, "Stories" quickly moved to Instagram, Facebook, Facebook Messenger, Twitter Fleets (2021 retired), LinkedIn, Pinterest, and YouTube (West 2021). Why so many Stories? Well, they are popular. In fact, 500 million people were using Instagram Stories in 2019 each day (McLachlan 2022).

While our visual storytelling discussion concentrates its efforts on static images and videos, GIFs, cinemagraphs, slides, and infographics are also increasingly popular image choices. In the social media sea of static images, marketers are embracing animated GIFs (i.e., graphics interchange format) and cinemagraphs (i.e., a photo and video combination where one or more image attributes seem alive through their movement) (Piekut 2015). Luxury brands, in particular, are drawn to cinemagraphs because of their ability to bring photos to life and allow them to articulate both beauty and sophistication in their visual storytelling. Both GIFs and cinemagraphs can be used on websites, e-mail, ads, and embedded within social media posts. Animated GIFs and cinemagraphs boast higher rates of engagement and conversion than static images (King 2016; Johnson 2015; Piekut 2015). However, they are not alone—although waning in popularity, infographics have also demonstrated strong virality (Dugan 2012). Finally, we would be remiss if we did not mention the incredible popularity of Slideshare. Infographics on Slideshare are also liked and shared considerably more than other documents and presentations (Abramovich 2014). Whereas this chapter does not include a detailed discussion on GIFs, cinemagraphs, slides, or infographics, much of the following discussion of visual storytelling is also applicable to these forms of visuals.

Visual Storytelling Is Not an Option

Visual assets' ability to increase engagement rates and influence purchases has forced companies to acknowledge their worth. A CMO Council and Libris sponsored survey of 177 senior marketing executives found that 65 percent of those surveyed believed that visual assets, in general, are essential in telling the story of their brand (CMO Council and Libris 2015). Forty-six percent of those surveyed believe that photos were "critical" in marketing and storytelling strategies, followed by video (36 percent), infographics (19 percent), and illustrations (15 percent). They also believe that visual asset use and importance will continue to grow (CMO Council and Libris 2015). Marketers consider their brand editorial images to be the most important in crafting their marketing strategy, followed by consumer-generated images, then brand stock images, influencer images, and finally, partner images (Curalate and Internet Marketing Association 2015). In other words, a combination of company, consumer, and collaborative content is important for telling your brand story.

While some social media platforms are dominated by company-generated images (i.e., Pinterest), most rely heavily on consumer-generated images. Consumers are actively creating and posting their visuals and sharing those created by other consumers on social media. Both company- and consumer-generated images work to influence consumer decision making, but consumer-generated content also influences marketers. For example, Pinterest boards were a source of design inspiration for the automotive company Buick (Gupta 2013). Engagement with images can be used to predict in-store and onsite product engagement, and consumer photos are now selected for inclusion in branded websites' homepages, fan galleries, and even product-landing pages (Curalate n.d.).

A recurring theme in this book is that consumers and marketers must work collaboratively within the social space. Marketers need to not only continue to encourage engagement from consumers but also actively integrate their content. Visual marketing firm Curalate recommends the 80/20 principle in your visual integration strategy: 80 percent of visuals should be generated by a company, whereas 20 percent should be "outsourced" to consumers and influencers, advocates, and so on (consumer and collaborative). How do we find consumer content to incorporate into our marketing?

Visual Analytics and Commerce

To find and then utilize visually oriented consumer-generated content requires new marketing solutions—enter visual intelligence and analytical tools and visual commerce. Historically, social media analytics have relied solely on textual analysis, ignoring the content of the image itself. As a result, approximately 85 percent of a brand's photos are "lost" because the brand is not mentioned in a post's text (Laughlin 2016). Companies, such as YouScan, Visua, and Crimson Hexagon, are using logo recognition software to analyze millions of social images to identify brand logos that are contained anywhere within a photo (e.g., on a cup, shoe, billboard) or even in a video or GIF. The logo may not even be the image's focal point; however, understanding the number of visual mentions within the social realm indicates a brand's popularity and media impact. It also allows marketers to discover affinities with other brands and general types of product relationships that they may not have known existed. In essence, visual analytics contextualizes and shows *how* consumers are using your product. Capturing the organic visual sWOM conversations allows the marketer to find and target consumers that have previously gone unnoticed, develop new products based on discovering new or unknown usage behavior, forge new marketing partnerships with affiliate brands, and understand which promotional materials are working. Some of the visual analytical tools also help you to identify and help connect with frequent brand posters or influencers and their social network.

Visual commerce is defined as:

> The full-funnel approach used in making all of the images both within and outside of a brand's control actionable at every point of the customer journey. This is accomplished by directly linking images to the products or services associated with them, resulting in traffic, conversions, and revenue. (Curalate and Internet Marketing Association 2015)

Visual commerce is a growing area. It allows an image to become a point of purchase. In other words, images have become shoppable. Consumers can click on a specific product in an image and be taken to an e-commerce platform to purchase it. One image can provide multiple purchasing opportunities. No longer are brand purchases limited to following a link in the brand's social media bio. Social media technology has evolved. To illustrate, Instagram allows "product tags" where brands can place clickable tags on their product posts and ads. One hundred and thirty million people click on Instagram shopping tags each month (Instagram 2022)! Instagram also includes a "Shop Tab" on the home screen to allow consumers to find additional products to purchase. Not to be outdone, Pinterest includes Product Pins that either direct users to a retailer's website or some products can be purchased within the Pinterest platform. TikTok also includes an in-app shopping experience. Creators can include a shopping tab to their profile which is connected to a creator's Shopify product catalog.

And, while we now have analytical tools that allow us to analyze photos and visual commerce tools that allow us to make purchases through images, we still do not know the answer to the question …

What Images or Video to Use?

What types of images or videos are consumers more likely to share? If you did not know already, more than likely it is not going to be an image solely of your product (remember: tell, not sell). Do not worry; your product can be part of the image, but there needs to be a positive context and perhaps a friendly face captured in it as well. The type of image or video that is shared is going to depend on the social media platform.

Consumers post a wide variety of images on Instagram. One study identified eight separate categories of Instagram images: friends (i.e., two human faces in the photo), food, gadgets (i.e., electronics, transportation), captioned photos, pets, activity (i.e., concert, landmark), selfies, and fashion (i.e., clothing, shoes, and so on). The most frequent categories of images posted (consisting of almost half of the data set of photos combined) were friends and selfies. The least frequent were pets and fashion (Hu, Manikonda, and Kambhampati 2014). In contrast, images posted on Pinterest *without* faces received 23 percent more repins than those that included faces (Curalate and Internet Marketing Association 2015). This difference can perhaps be attributed to the varying motives beyond using the social network; Pinterest is more about "things" and Instagram is more about "people."

Video communication provides a much richer communication platform, and arguably, it is harder to pinpoint, let alone create content that can be contagious. However, a content analysis of videos collected from the UK does yield some suggestions. In a study of 800 user-generated and branded social videos, researchers Nelson-Field, Riebe, and Sharp (2013) looked at the average rate of sharing each day, aggregated by the type of creative devices used in the video. The most popular creative device use (by a considerable amount) was personal triumph, followed by weather, science, or nature and baby or young child (remember the popular "Charlie Bit My Finger" video?).

Image Attributes

From the time we opened up our first Crayola box, color has fascinated us. And, we all have our favorite. Color can capture attention, generate emotions, and symbolize ideas. Its effects are both physiological and psychological. And, importantly for marketing, color impacts consumer decision making. But, does color impact sharing behavior within social media?

Research has readily shown that blue (across cultures) is most often selected as the favorite color, and this preference is also seen online (at least on Instagram). Visual marketing firm Curalate's study of more than 8 million Instagram images found that when blue is the dominant color in an Instagram image, it attracts 24 percent more likes than an image that is predominately red and orange (Dixit 2013). However, this was not found to be the case on Pinterest, where images that contain red, orange, and brown are repinned approximately twice as often as images containing blue images (Lowry 2013). A separate study also found that red and related shades (e.g., pink and purple) increased repinning behavior, whereas black, yellow, yellow-green, green, and blue deterred it (Bakhshi and Gilbert 2015). Instead of focusing on one color within Pinterest, multiple colors might be a better approach. On Pinterest, repinning was 3.25 times higher when an image contained multiple colors as opposed to one dominant (Lowry 2013).

Levels of brightness and saturation are other considerations when posting images. On Pinterest, "medium" lightness is best for repinning (Lowry 2013), whereas "high lightness" attracts considerably more likes than dark images on Instagram (Dixit 2013). The background of the image can also make a difference in liking and sharing. On Pinterest, images containing relatively little white space (i.e., less than 30 percent) were repinned at higher rates (Lowry 2013). In contrast, Instagram images with a lot of backgrounds were liked more often (Dixit 2013). Even the texture of an image, determined by the number of edges, makes a difference on Pinterest. Smooth texture images (think rounded surfaces) are repinned at considerably higher rates than images that have many rough edges (Lowry 2013). The opposite was found within Instagram, where a lot of texture led to considerably more likes (Dixit 2013). Unfortunately, color selection is not a black and white decision (pun intended), nor will one color be the answer for higher engagement. Social media colors are impacted by the brand's colors and also the specific product category of the brand. An analysis of over 200,000 Instagram fashion images found significant color-related engagement differences between different types of fashion (i.e., casual wear did well with purple; footwear did well with black). It is, however, not easy to be green. Posts featuring green, across fashion categories, didn't perform well (Nanji 2018).

Phew! That is a lot of information to digest. So, we helped you out by summarizing this information in Figure 4.3. We added text and images, but unfortunately, we were unable to add color, video, or sound.

So, have you figured out your big brand story? Will it be textually and visually rich? Even when you have written your tale, the next hurdle you face is figuring out how you will use it to drive action. In other words, how will you influence others within social media?

Keys to Successful Storytelling

Character: The characters in your story should be someone that your consumers can relate to and are perceived to be credible.
"Big" brand story idea: The story should be simple and get at the core of your brand's identity.
Story arc: Brand stories are a collection of information or posts—not told in one sitting. Each story presents a hurdle or challenge that must be overcome.
Story execution: Execute your story on social media platforms your consumers use and know. Make sure your story fits with the platform.
Brand voice: Text and visually oriented posts must be consistent; consistent between posts and with the brand image or story.
Coauthor (with consumers): Nurture and encourage consumers to tell stories.

Story Content

Post content that your consumers value:
Social currency: Content that helps your consumers improve their digital identity.
Triggers: Content that aligns with current events, activities, and obstacles.
Public: Content that stands out and can be easily identified with your company.
Practical value: Content that is useful.
Stories: Content that tells small stories that work to support the bigger story themes.
Emotions: Content that create high arousal, e.g., awe, excitement, humor, and anger.

Creative Strategies

Choose the right appeal.
Invite consumers to contribute content.
Offer an incentive.
Focus on telling, not selling.

Textual Storytelling

Shorter is often better. However, this varies by platform.
Use acronyms that consumers understand and have been known to use.
Word selection (simple vs. sophisticated) and length (short vs. long) should be based on the characteristics of your intended audience.
Use verbs, positive adjectives, subject and object pronouns.
When using a call-to-action say "Please."
Include URL links.
Limit your use of hashtags. Make them unique.

Visual Storytelling

Visual storytelling is not an option.
Consumers are more likely to remember images than text.
Recall is greater for images that evoke high emotional arousals.
Use filters to make photos fun and unique.
Choose colors carefully to evoke emotion.
Gifs, cinemagraphs, slides, and infographics are good storytelling tools.
Use videos to create and tell short stories.
Use a combination of company, consumer, and collaborative content.
Be conscious of the type of content that consumers expect to see on a given platform. E.g., Pinterest—things, Instagram—people.

Figure 4.3 Storytelling

References

Aaker, D.A. and D. Norris. 1982. "Characteristics of TV Commericals Perceived as Informative." *Journal of Advertising Research* 22, no. 2, pp. 61–70.

Abramovich, G. 2014. "15 Mind-Blowing Stats About Slideshare." *CMO*. Retrieved from www.cmo.com/features/articles/2014/3/10/mind_blowing_stats_slideshare.html#gs.jAcOvsA.

Advanced Marketing Institute. 2009. "Emotional Marketing Value Headline Analyzer." Retrieved from www.aminstitute.com/headline/index.htm.

Ashley, C. and T. Tuten. 2015. "Creative Strategies in Social Media Marketing: An Exploratory Study of Branded Social Content and Consumer Engagement." *Psychology and Marketing* 32, no. 1, pp. 15–27.

ASKfm. 2022. "A, Bae, C's: Top Teen Terms Decoded." *ASKfm blog*. Retrieved from https://safety.ask.fm/a-bae-cs-top-teen-terms-decoded/.

Bakhshi, S. and E. Gilbert. 2015. "Red, Purple and Pink: The Colors of Diffusion on Pinterest." *PLoS One* 10, no. 2, p. e011718. Retrieved from https://journals.plos.org/plosone/article?id=10.1371/journal.pone.0117148.

Bakhshi, S., D. Shamma, L. Kennedy, and E. Gilbert. 2014. "Why We Filter Our Photos and How It Impacts Engagement." In *International AAAI Conference on Human Factors in Computing Systems,* pp. 12–22. http://comp.social.gatech.edu/papers/icwsm15.why.bakhshi.pdf.

Bennett, S. 2014a. "The History of Hashtags in Social Media Marketing." *AdWeek*. Retrieved from www.adweek.com/socialtimes/history-hashtag-social-marketing/501237.

Bennett, S. 2014b. "U.S. Social Commerce—Statistics & Trends." *AdWeek*. Retrieved from www.adweek.com/socialtimes/social-commerce-stats-trends/500895?red=at.

Berger, J. 2013. *Contagious*. New York, NY: Simon and Schuster.

Berger, J. and K. Milkman. 2011. "What Makes Online Content Viral?" *Journal of Marketing Research* 49, no. 2, pp. 192–205.

Bly, B. 2013. "A New Copywriting Formula: The 4 Cs." *IBPA*. Retried from https://articles.ibpa-online.org/article/a-new-copywriting-formula-the-4-cs/#:~:text=A%20copywriting%20formula%20I%20use,concise%2C%20compelling%2C%20and%20credible.

Bone, P. 1995. "Word-of-Mouth Effects on Short-Term and Long-Term Product Judgments." *Journal of Business Research* 32, no. 3, pp. 213–23.

Brown, J. and P. Reingen. 1987. "Social Ties and Word-of-Mouth Referral Behavior." *Journal of Consumer Research* 14, no. 3, pp. 350–362.

Bullas, J. 2012. "6 Powerful Reasons Why You Should Include Images in Your Marketing." *Jeffbullas.com*. Retrieved from www.jeffbullas.com/2012/05/28/6-powerful-reasons-why-you-should-include-images-in-your-marketing-infographic/.

Childers, T.L. and M.J. Houston. 1984. "Conditions for a Picture-Superiority Effect on Consumer Memory." *Journal of Consumer Research* 11, no. 2, pp. 643–53.

Cisco. 2016. "VNI Complete Forecast Highlights." *Cisco*. Retrieved from www.cisco.com/c/dam/m/en_us/solutions/service-provider/vni-forecast-highlights/pdf/Global_2021_Forecast_Highlights.pdf.

CMO Council and Libris. 2015. "From Creativity to Content: The Role of Visual Media in Impactful Brand Storytelling." Retrieved from https://d3kjp0zrek7zit.cloudfront.net/uploads/attachment/file/42928/expirable-direct-uploads_2F09469a4a-87fa-43c8-afe4-a71d013c5bcb_2FCMO-Council_PhotoShelter_Whitepaper_Final.pdf.

Coca-Cola. 2021a. "Coca-Cola Launches 'Real Magic' Brand Platform Including Refreshed Visual Identity and Global Campaign." Retrieved from www.coca-colacompany.com/news/coca-cola-launches-real-magic-brand-platform-including-refreshed-visual-identity-and-global-campaign.

Coca-Cola. 2021b. "Coca-Cola Launches New Christmas Campaign Under 'Real Magic' Platform." Retrieved from www.coca-colacompany.com/news/real-magic-christmas-campaign.

Content Marketing Institute. n.d. "What Is Content Marketing." Retrieved from http://contentmarketinginstitute.com/what-is-content-marketing/ (accessed July 31, 2016).

Contently. 2016. "The Content Marketing Encyclopedia." Retrieved from https://contently.com/strategist/2016/06/29/content-marketing-101-art-storytelling-webinar/ (accessed July 31, 2016).

Courie, E. 2021. "Exclusive: Coca-Cola Brings 'Real Magic' in First New Campaign Since 2016." *Biz Community*. Retrieved from www.bizcommunity.com/Article/196/11/222738.html.

Cucu, E. 2022. "2022 Social Media Industry Benchmarks." *Social Insider Blog*. Retrieved from www.socialinsider.io/blog/social-media-industry-benchmarks/.

Curalate. n.d. "The Complete Guide to Visual Commerce: How to Command Attention in a Visual Words." Retrieved from http://pages.curalate.com/the-complete-visual-commerce-guide.html.

Curalate and Internet Marketing Association. 2015. "The State of Visual Commerce." Retrieved from http://pages.curalate.com/rs/496-DAU-231/images/The_State_of_Visual_Commerce.pdf.

Daugherty, T. and E. Hoffman. 2014. "eWOM and the Importance of Capturing Consumer Attention Within Social Media." *Journal of Marketing Communications* 20, no. 1–2, pp. 82–102. doi:10.1080/13527266.2013.797764.

Dixit, P. 2013. "Want Your Instagram Photos to Get Attention? Use the Color Blue." *Fast Company*. Retrieved from www.fastcompany.com/3021407/want-your-instagram-photos-to-get-attention-use-the-color-blue.

Domo. 2021. "Data Never Sleeps 9.0." *Domo Resources*. Retrieved from www.domo.com/learn/infographic/data-never-sleeps-9.

Dugan, L. 2012. "Infographics Shared on Twitter Get 832% More Retweets Than Images and Articles." *Adweek*. Retrieved from www.adweek.com/socialtimes/infographics-on-twitter/468324.

ElBoghdady, D. April 20, 2012. "'Pink Slime' Outrage Goes Viral in Stunning Display of Social Media's Power." *The Washington Post*. Retrieved from https://www.washingtonpost.com/business/pink-slime-outrage-goes-viral-in-stunning-display-of-social-medias-power/2012/04/20/gIQAIf5XVT_story.html

Elliot, N. 2015. "How Does Your Brand Stack Up on Facebook, Twitter and Instagram?" *Forrester: Nate Elliott's Blog*. Retrieved from www.forrester.com/blogs/15-09-15-how_does_your_brand_stack_up_on_facebook_twitter_and_instagram/.

Elliot, S. November 11, 2012. "Coke Revamps Website to Tell Its Story." *The New York Times*. Retrieved from www.nytimes.com/2012/11/12/business/media/coke-revamps-web-site-to-tell-its-story.html?_r=0.

Eveleth, R. n.d. "How Many Photographs of You Are Out There in the World?" *The Atlantic*. Retrieved from www.theatlantic.com/technology/archive/2015/11/how-many-photographs-of-you-are-out-there-in-the-world/413389/.

Felder, R.M. and L.K. Silberman. 1988. "Learning and Teaching Styles." *Engineering Education* 78, no. 7, pp. 67–81.

Fernandez, M. 2020. "700+ Power Words That Will Boost Your Conversions." *Optinmonster Blog*. Retrieved from https://optinmonster.com/700-power-words-that-will-boost-your-conversions/.

Gessler, K. 2020. "Twitter Length Study: Do Longer Tweets Drive More Engagement and Referral Traffic." *Kurt Gessler Blog*. Retrieved from https://kurtgessler.medium.com/twitter-length-study-do-longer-tweets-drive-more-engagement-and-referral-traffic-3dd0781363ff.

Grady, D. 1993. "The Vision Thing: Mainly in the Brain." *Discover*. Retrieved from http://discovermagazine.com/1993/jun/thevisionthingma227.

Grass, R.C. and U.H. Wallace. 1974. "Advertising Communication: Print vs. TV." *Journal of Advertising Research* 14, no. 5, pp. 19–23.

Guido, M. 2016. "10 Brutal Trend and Campaign Hashtag Fails + Lessons to Learn From Them." Keyhole. Retrieved from http://keyhole.co/blog/10-trend-campaign-hashtag-fails-by-big-brands-lessons/.

Gunelius, S. 2013. "5 Secrets to Use Storytelling for Brand Marketing Success." *Forbes*. Retrieved from www.forbes.com/sites/work-in-progress/2013/02/05/5-secrets-to-using-storytelling-for-brand-marketing-success/#1e344bfa3dd9.

Gupta, A. 2013. "The Shift From Words to Pictures and Implications for Digital Marketers." *Forbes*. Retrieved from www.forbes.com/sites/onmarketing/2013/07/02/the-shift-from-words-to-pictures-and-implications-for-digital-marketers/#586b936c2549.

Hoffman, E. and T. Daugherty. 2013. "Is a Picture Always Worth a Thousand Words? Attention to Structural Elements of Ewom for Consumer Brands

Within Social Media." In *Advances in Consumer Research*, eds. S. Botti and A. Labroo. Association for Consumer Research. www.acrwebsite.org/volumes/v41/acr_v41_14817.pdf.

Hu, Y., L. Manikonda, and S. Kambhampati. 2014. "What We Instagram: A First Analysis of Instagram Photo Content and User Types." In *Proceedings of the 8th International AAAI Conference on Weblogs and Social Media*. Association for Advancement of Artificial Intelligence. Retrieved from www.aaai.org/ocs/index.php/ICWSM/ICWSM14/paper/view/8118/8087.

Hutchinson, A. 2019. "New Report Looks at Optimal Facebook Posting Practices in 2019." *Social Media Today*. Retrieved from www.socialmediatoday.com/news/new-report-looks-at-optimal-facebook-posting-practices-in-2019/545233/.

Instagram. 2022. "Shopping." Retrieved from https://about.instagram.com/features/shopping.

Johnson, L. 2015. "Here's Why GIFs Are Back in Style and Bigger Than Ever for Brands: Creators Race for Marketers' 'Loopy' Business." *Adweek*. Retrieved from www.adweek.com/news/technology/heres-why-gifs-are-back-style-and-bigger-ever-brands-165499.

Kagan, N. 2017. "How to Create Viral Content: 10 Insights From 100 Million Articles." *OkDork*. Retrieved from https://okdork.com/why-content-goes-viral-what-analyzing-100-millions-articles-taught-us/.

King, C. 2016. "5 Ways to Use Cinemagraphs in Digital Marketing Campaigns." *Flixel Blog*. Retrieved from http://blog.flixel.com/5-ways-to-use-cinemagraphs-in-digital-marketing-campaigns/.

Kitroeff, N. and J. Lorin. 2015. "Students Bombed the SAT This Year, in Four Charts." *Bloomberg*. Retrieved from www.bloomberg.com/news/articles/2015-09-03/students-bombed-the-sat-this-year-in-four-charts.

Kozinets, R.V., K. De Valck, A.C. Wojnicki, and S.J.S. Wilner. 2010. "Networked Narratives: Understanding Word-of-Mouth Marketing in Online Communities." *Journal of Marketing* 74, no. 2, pp. 71–89.

Kremer, W. 2015. "Are Humans Getting Cleverer?" *BBC News*. www.bbc.com/news/magazine-31556802.

Laskey, H., E. Day, and M. Crask. 1989. "Typology of Main Message Strategies for Television Commercials." *Journal of Advertising* 18, no. 1, pp. 36–41.

Laughlin, S. 2016. "Q& A: David Rose, CEO, Ditto Labs." *J. Walter Thompson Intelligence*. Retrieved from www.jwtintelligence.com/2016/03/david-rose-ceo-ditto-labs/.

Lewsey, F. n.d. "Slamming Political Rivals May Be the Most Effective Way to Go Viral—Revealing Social Media's 'Perverse Incentives.'" *University of Cambridge Stories*. Retrieved from www.cam.ac.uk/stories/viralpolitics.

Libert, K. 2014. "Here's What 2.7 Billion Social Shares Say About Content Marketing." *Marketingland*. Retrieved from http://marketingland.com/heres-2-7-billion-social-shares-say-state-online-publishing-99572.

Lieb, R., J. Groopman, and C. Li. 2014. "The Content Marketing Software Landscape: Marketer Needs and Vendor Solutions." Retrieved from https://rebeccalieb.com/sites/default/files/downloads/1406%20Content%20Marketing%20Software%20Landscape%20RL.pdf.

Linehan, L., S. Rayson, and H. Chiu. 2021. "100m Articles Analyzed: What You Need to Know to Write the Best Headlines." *BuzzSumo Blog*. Retrieved from https://buzzsumo.com/blog/most-shared-headlines-study/#section-66.

Lowry, B. 2013. "Beautify Your Content: 8 Image Features That Shine on Pinterest." *Curalate Blog*. Retrieved from www.curalate.com/blog/8-image-features-that-shine-on-pinterest/.

McLachlan, S. 2022. "35 Instagram Stats That Matter to Marketers in 2022." *Hootsuite Blog*. Retrieved from https://blog.hootsuite.com/instagram-statistics/.

Meeker, M. 2016. "Internet Trends 2016—Code Conference." Retrieved from www.kleinerperkins.com/perspectives/2016-internet-trends-report/.

Moon, G. 2014. "Make Your Content More Sharable With These Simple Tricks, Backed by Research." *Buffer*. Retrieved from https://blog.bufferapp.com/shareable-content-social-media-research.

Moore, R. 2012. "Pinterest Data Analysis: An Inside Look." *The Datapoint*. Retrieved from https://blog.rjmetrics.com/2012/02/15/pinterest-data-analysis-an-inside-look/.

Murphy, S. 2012. "How to Get More Likes, Shares on Facebook." *Mashable*. Retrieved from http://mashable.com/2012/06/19/how-to-get-more-likes-shares-on-facebook-infographic/#SrvzU.0Boiqt.

Nanji, A. 2018. "How Color Impacts Fashion Brands' Instagram Engagement." *Marketing Profs*. Retrieved from www.marketingprofs.com/charts/2018/33544/how-color-impacts-fashion-brands-instagram-engagement.

Nelson-Field, K., E. Riebe, and B. Sharp. 2013. "Emotions and Sharing." In *Viral Marketing: The Science of Sharing*, eds. K. Nelson-Field and B. Sharp, pp. 13–32. South Melbourne, Australia: Oxford University Press.

Nelson-Field, K., J. Taylor, and N. Hartnett. 2013. "The Pay Off." In *Viral Marketing: The Science of Sharing*, eds. K. Nelson-Field and B. Sharp, pp. 69–78. South Melbourne, Australia: Oxford University Press.

O'Brien, J. 2012. "How Red Bull Takes Content Marketing to the Extreme." *Mashable*. Retrieved from http://mashable.com/2012/12/19/red-bull-content-marketing/#oBPQRljrL5qN.

Paivio, A., T.B. Rogers, and P. Smythe. 1968. "Why Are Pictures Easier to Recall Than Words?" *Psychonomic Science* 11, no. 4, pp. 137–38.

Park, C. and T.M. Lee. 2009. "Information Direction, Website Reputation and the eWOM Effect: A Moderating Role of Product Type." *Journal of Business Research* 62, no. 1, pp. 61–67.

Patel, N. 2014. "What Type of Content Gets Shared the Most on Twitter." *Quicksprout Blog*. Retrieved from www.quicksprout.com/2014/03/05/what-type-of-content-gets-shared-the-most-on-twitter/.

Pensiero, K. September 11, 2015. "Alylan Kurdi and the Photos That Change History." *The Washington Street Journal*. Retrieved from www.wsj.com/articles/aylan-kurdi-and-the-photos-that-change-history-1442002594.

Pfeffer, J., T. Zorbach, and K.M. Carley. 2014. "Understanding Online Firestorms: Negative Word-of-Mouth Dynamics in Social Media Networks." *Journal of Marketing Communications* 20, no. 1–2, pp. 117–128. doi:10.1080/13527266.2013.797778.

Piekut, K. 2015. "How Cinemagraphs Are Helping Brands Break Away From Static Content." *Econslutancy Blog*. Retrieved from https://econsultancy.com/blog/66568-how-cinemagraphs-are-helping-brands-break-away-from-static-content/.

Pieters, R. and M. Wedel. 2004. "Attention Capture and Transfer in Adverting: Brand, Pictorial, and Text-Size Effects." *Journal of Marketing* 68, no. 2, pp. 36–50.

Queensland University of Technology. 2020. "Seeing no longer Believing: The Manipulation of Online Images." *Science Daily*. Retrieved from www.sciencedaily.com/releases/2020/10/201021112337.htm.

Quicksprout. 2021. "How to Increase Twitter Engagement by 324%." *Quicksprout Blog*. Retrieved from www.quicksprout.com/twitter-engagement/.

Quintly. 2019. "Instagram Study 2019." *Quintly*. Retrieved from https://info.quintly.com/instagram-study-2019/view#length.

Richins, M.L. 1983. "Negative Word-of-Mouth by Dissatisfied Consumers: A Pilot Study." *Journal of Marketing* 47, no. 1, pp. 68–78.

Ripen Ecommerce. 2014. "Adding Pinterest to Your Ecommerce Strategy." Retrieved from www.ripenecommerce.com/blog/pinterest-for-ecommerce.

Rogers, S. 2014. "What Fuels a Tweet's Engagement." *Twitter Blog*. https://blog.twitter.com/2014/what-fuels-a-tweets-engagement.

Romanek, J. 2013. "Tweet Tips: Most Effective Calls to Action on Twitter." *Twitter Blog*. Retrieved from https://blog.twitter.com/2013/tweet-tips-most-effective-calls-to-action-on-twitter.

Shaer, M. 2014. "What Emotion Goes Viral the Fastest." *Smithsonian*. Retrieved from www.smithsonianmag.com/science-nature/what-emotion-goes-viral-fastest-180950182/?no-ist.

Shopify. 2016. "How Pinterest Drives Online Commerce." Retrieved from www.shopify.com/infographics/pinterest (accessed August 15, 2016).

Singh, S.N., P.V. Lessig, D. Kim, R. Gupta, and M.A. Hocutt. 2000. "Does Your Ad Have Too Many Pictures?" *Journal of Advertising Research* 40, no. 1, pp. 11–27.

Snow, S. 2015. "State of Content Marketing 2016: The Tipping Point." *Contently*. Retrieved from https://contently.com/strategist/2015/12/17/state-of-content-marketing-2016/.

Stenberg, G. 2006. "Conceptual and Perceptual Factors in the Picture Superiority Effect." *European Journal of Cognitive Psychology* 18, no. 6, pp. 813–47.

Stich, L., G. Golla, and A. Nanopoulos. 2014. "Modelling the Spread of Negative Word-of-Mouth in Online Social Networks." *Journal of Decision Systems* 23, no. 2. pp. 230–21. doi:10.1080/12460125.2014.886494.

Tierney, J. February 08, 2010. "Will You Be E-Mailing This Column? It's Awesome." *The New York Times*. Retrieved from www.nytimes.com/2010/02/09/science/09tier.html.

Toms. 2022. "Toms Impact Report 2021." Retrieved from www.toms.com/us/impact/report.html.

Warren, J. 2021. "Instagram Hashtags: Everything You Need to Know in 2022." *Later Blog*. Retrieved from https://later.com/blog/ultimate-guide-to-using-instagram-hashtags/.

Werner, K.R. 1984. "Effects of Emotional Pictorial Elements in Ads Analyzed by Means of Eye Movement Monitoring." In *Advances in Consumer Research*, ed. T. Kinnear, pp. 591–596. Association for Consumer Research. www.acrwebsite.org/volumes/6313/volumes/v11/NA-11.

West, C. 2021. "Social Media Stories: Your Guide to All Social Media Story Platforms." *Sprout Blog*. Retrieved from https://sproutsocial.com/insights/social-media-stories/.

Zarrella, D. 2009. "The Science of Retweets." Retrieved from www.slideshare.net/danzarrella/the-science-of-re-tweets/24-ReTweets_are_Social_and_Concrete.

Zarrella, D. 2012. "New Facebook Data Proves Social CTAs Lead to More Comments, Likes & Shares." *HubSpot*. Retrieved from http://blog.hubspot.com/blog/tabid/6307/bid/33860/New-Facebook-Data-Proves-Social-CTAs-Lead-to-More-Comments-Likes-Shares-INFOGRAPHIC.aspx#sm.00018n9uis1172fifrc4xqq28xm0f.

Zarrella, D. 2013a. "New Data Shows the 7 Most Powerful Calls-to-Actions for More Retweets." *Dan Zarrella*. Retrieved from http://danzarrella.com/new-data-shows-the-7-most-powerful-calls-to-action-for-more-retweets/ (accessed February 08, 2017).

Zarrella, D. 2013b. "Use 'Quotes' and #Hashtags to Get More Retweets." *Dan Zarrella*. Retrieved from http://danzarrella.com/new-data-use-quotes-and-hashtags-to-get-more-retweets/ (accessed February 08, 2017).

Zarrella, D. 2014. "The Science of Instagram." *Dan Zarrella*. Retrieved from http://danzarrella.com/infographic-the-science-of-instagram/ (accessed February 08, 2017).

Zote, Z. 2020. "130 Most Important Social Media Acronyms and Slang You Should Know." *Sprout Social Blog*. Retrieved from https://sproutsocial.com/insights/social-media-acronyms/.

CHAPTER 5

Social Influencers and Employee Advocates

In 2020, French luxury fashion house Dior utilized the service of influencer marketing agency Buttermilk to recruit 67 influencers across the globe. Dior hired these influencers to drive awareness and generate buzz around the new Dior Forever Foundation, a range of 67 unique foundation shades. The company matched influencers with the proper foundation for their skin tone, and each day for 67 consecutive days, a different influencer would post a photo wearing their appropriate shade. Collectively, the group reached a global audience of 2.66 million, created 1.85 million impressions (the number of times people viewed a piece of content), and 591 thousand points of engagement (interaction with a fan, such as a "share" or "like") (Single Grain 2021).

Influencer marketing is a method of advertising products and services via individuals with a dedicated social media following on popular platforms such as Instagram, YouTube, Facebook, TikTok, and Snapchat. These individuals are perceived to be credible sources of information and, therefore, persuasive marketers who can influence the purchase decisions of the followers (Rahal 2020). Influencers can help a business reach a bigger audience, increase website traffic, generate leads, drive sales, and help grow the business's social media following (Single Grain 2021). Influencers are often, but not always, third-party individuals. An influencer can also exist within the company. For example, a senior executive or employee with a specific area of expertise can be highly influential. This chapter explores the different types of influencers, beginning with paid external third-party social media influencers, followed by a discussion on those within the company who can effectively reach consumers—c-suite thought leaders and employee advocates. We will finish with a brief discussion of the importance of engaging with everyday consumers who support your brand.

External Influencers

The global social media influencer marketing industry is estimated to reach $15 billion in 2022, up from $1.7 billion in 2016 (Rahal 2020). Influencer marketing is a popular strategy for increasing sales (33.6 percent), building brand awareness (33.5 percent), and assisting in building a library of user-generated content (32.8 percent) (Influencer Marketing Hub 2021). A 2021 international survey of 5,000 brand representatives revealed that 75 percent had or planned to have a budget dedicated to influencer marketing. Ninety percent believed influencer marketing to be an effective form of marketing, with 62 percent planning to increase their funding. Thirty-eight percent expect to increase their budget by 10 to 20 percent (Influencer Marketing Hub 2021). Fifty-six percent of companies that have adopted influencer marketing work with the same influencers across different campaigns, indicating a preference to build a relationship with a select group of individuals. The most widely used social channels by social influencers in 2021 were Instagram (68 percent), TikTok (45 percent), and Facebook (43 percent) (Influencer Marketing Hub 2021).

Categories of Paid Social Influencers

Influencers are frequently classified according to the size of their following. There are five primary categories—mega influencers, macro-, mid-tier, micro-, and nano influencers (Different Types of Influencers: Mega, Macro, Micro and Nano 2020).

Mega Influencers

Mega influencers are individuals, often A-list celebrities (e.g., athletes, entertainers, actors) famous in real life for their talent or profession. They have over one million diverse followers on their social media channels, which helps generate awareness of mass-market appeal products (e.g., cars). However, these people have no real relationship with their followers. As a result, depending on the product, this group may not be instrumental in converting awareness to purchase. Mega influencers can also be expensive to hire and are often only suitable for big brands with big budgets. These influencers typically charge a minimum of $10,000 per post. Some, such as the artist Beyonce, can command over $1 million (Different Types of Influencers: Mega, Macro, Micro and Nano 2020).

Macro Influencers

Macro social media influencers usually have between 500,001 and 1 million followers. These individuals may have gained fame through the Internet. For example, they may have a popular YouTube channel or blog. Typically, macro influencers focus on a specific product category (e.g., video games, cosmetics, fitness) and are considered experts in their field. Unlike mega influencers, who view promoting products as a tiny part of their job, social media may be a full-time job for macro influencers. This influencer category is helpful for companies with a large consumer base (e.g., teenage girls and gamers). This influencer earns $5,000 to $10,000 for a single social media post.

Mid-Tier Influencers

Mid-tier influencers have attracted 50,001 to 500,000 social media followers. They are mildly successful and perhaps on the cusp of becoming famous. They are known for a specific product category (e.g., fashion). Despite their smaller following, they can be very effective at generating high levels of engagement and are best suited for campaigns with medium-sized budgets. These influencers earn $500 to $5,000 per post.

Micro Influencers

Micro influencers have followings in the 10,001 to 50,000 range. This group has a niche following, meaning their audience is more focused, perhaps around a specific industry or topic (e.g., travel or photography). Because of the size of their audience, micro influencers can interact with their followers regularly. This interaction helps build strong ties and positions the micro influencer as more relatable to their followers than some of the other categories. Whereas different categories of influencers can successfully generate mass awareness, micro influencers ability to create high levels of engagement can help drive consumers through the decision-making process closer to the purchase stage. This group is highly invested in creating their content, unlike other influencers that may rely on the company to supply content. For that reason, their posts may appear and feel more authentic. They earn $100 to $500 for each post.

Nano Influencers

Individuals with 1,000 to 10,000 followers are categorized as nano influencers. These are everyday people who have amassed a modest following of highly engaged people. These influencers likely have real-world relationships with a large number of their followers. An example of a nano influencer could be someone in your company, community, or within your circle of friends. Because they are essential "normal" people, they are more relatable, approachable, and considered the most authentic. They can be highly persuasive with their followers. Nano influencers are plentiful, easy to find, and inexpensive. They typically earn $10 to $100 per post.

Identifying and Hiring Influencers

As the popularity of influencer marketing grows, so too does the number of agencies and platforms offering services to help companies identify and recruit influencers and manage their campaigns. During 2015 and 2020, the number of influencer-focused agencies and platforms grew from 335 to 1360. Platforms such as UpInfluence, IZEA, and Intellifluence allow companies to discover and interact with suitable influencers. Companies can search for influencers, automate campaigns, pay influencers, and measure success all from one platform.

Despite the availability of agency support, the preference for many companies is to run influencer campaigns in-house (77 percent) (Influencer Marketing Hub 2021). Whether a company chooses to utilize an agency, a platform, or manage the entire campaign in-house, they need to think carefully about the category or categories of influencers that are the most appropriate given the goals they have set for their campaign.

The importance of identifying and creating relationships with influencers is well established. In truth, recognizing "the right" influencers is one of the most challenging tasks. When evaluating potential candidates, four factors should be considered—relevance, risk, reach, and resonance.

- Relevance is how well the influencer aligns with your brand. Does the influencer have the expertise and subject-matter credibility with your target market? Are they already using your product? Do their values align with those of your company? Influencers must share your market's same values, culture, and demographics. The essential factor here is to ensure the characteristics of their followers are similar to those of your target market.
- Risk refers to the potential for the influencer to make a social media post that could harm your brand's reputation and image. Does an influencer have political beliefs that are not in line with your brand's values? Are visual and language choices not "on-brand" for your company? How have they historically engaged with their followers? Ultimately, when you form a relationship with an influencer you are providing an endorsement. Their bad actions will, therefore, be interrupted as your company's bad actions.
- Reach is the number of followers that the influencer has within one or more of their social platforms. The larger the following, the greater the number of people that will be potentially exposed to the message. The influencer will need to be active and have a significant following on the same platforms your target consumers use. Also, the larger the following, the higher the cost. Do you have the budget to support this level of influencer?
- Resonance refers to the degree of engagement that consumers have with the influencer. When the influencer posts content, what is the level of engagement? Do they receive a significant number of likes, shares, and comments? Are they going to amplify your message to a broader audience successfully? If you subscribe to one of the influencer platforms mentioned

earlier, they will provide data that will help you evaluate the relevance, risk, reach, and resonance. If you are not, you will need to research potential hires before entering into a formal relationship.

Structuring Influencers Programs and Compensation

Marketers need to approach a relationship with a potential influencer like a new budding friendship. As such, rules of "normal," real-life relationships are still applicable in this context: get to know them, be a good listener, and be respectful. Brands that follow and actively engage with an influencer before they recruit them are more likely to be successful. Ultimately, collaboration is the key when working with an influencer. Marketers need to meet with influencers and provide them with sample content and a general outline of their story—but influencers need to have input, "skin in the game"—because it is *their playground* you are asking your brand to play on. In truth, you are approaching an influencer because you want to capitalize on their preexisting consumer relationships. You also rely on their communication and content expertise within specific social media platforms (Maoz 2016a). Following is a list of items adapted from Klear's influencer informational guidelines for you to share with the influencer (Maoz 2016b).

- Company and product overview: You should educate them about the company and the product if they are not already familiar with the brand.
- Campaign overview: Provide them with a description of the campaign, its objectives, theme, applicable hashtags, and URL links.
- Creative: Outline the key messaging points you are looking for, highlight great examples of posts the influencer has previously done, and identify other social media posts consistent with the creative approach you would like to see. In some cases, you may want to offer some creative materials for them to use.
- Social media platforms: Identity the platforms where you would ideally like to see the influencer post.

- Content volume and disclosure: Identify the preferred number and frequency of posting. Also, explicitly state your method of disclosure.

While creative freedom is good, it is essential to create explicit guidelines and a firm contract stating your goals and expectations (Maoz 2016a). Specifying the frequency of posts is the first step in having some control. The most common sponsored posting durations are more than once a week and two or three times a month (Halverson Group 2015). It is also important to clearly explain any legal or regulatory issues they must abide by, including meeting the FTC (Federal Trade Commission) guidelines for disclosing a material connection between them and your brand. We will cover this in Chapter 7.

In terms of compensation, a global study revealed that 36 percent of companies surveyed preferred offering payment in the form of free samples, which is a common strategy for those employing nano- and micro influencers. A further 32.4 percent provided monetary compensation, with the remaining 21 percent offering discounts and 10.5 percent providing entry into a giveaway (Influencer Marketing Hub 2021). Not surprisingly, as a company's investment in influencer marketing grows, so too does the importance of being able to measure outcomes and show a healthy return on your investment.

Measuring Social Influencer Success

The metric that you will use to measure the return on your investment is tied to the goals you set. What was the purpose of implementing an influencer campaign? Was it to increase awareness of your brand? Drive more traffic to your website? Generate more sales? The most popular measures of ROI are conversion sales (38.5 percent), and increased social media engagement, including click-throughs (32.5 percent), followed by increased visibility measured by views/reach/impression (29 percent) (Influencer Marketing Hub 2021).

A straightforward approach to measuring click-throughs is through the use of URLs. Each social influencer is provided with a unique URL to include in their posting. Website analytics tools such as Google Analytics,

Adobe Analytics, and Angelfish Actual Metrics can track where your site visitors originated from (e.g., clicked on a link in an Instagram post). Having a unique URL for each influencer makes it easy to tie the traffic and any subsequent sale to a specific influencer. You can create a unique URL using UTM (Urchin Traffic Monitor) parameters. A UTM parameter is a string of code placed at the end of a URL to define the source, medium, campaign, term, and content that directed the consumer to your website. There are five parameters that can be added to the end of each link.

Source content: The source or platform driving the traffic, for example, Facebook.

Medium: This allows you to specify the medium which captured the user's attention, for example, promoted tweet, video, or display ad.

Campaign: If the content is tied to a specific campaign, you can add the name or descriptor for the campaign. This can be particularly helpful if multiple campaigns are being promoted simultaneously (e.g., floral dress or summer hat). Alternatively, you could use the name of the influencer (e.g., JaneD).

Terms: This parameter is added when running an advertising campaign where you may have paid for keywords or search terms (e.g., free shipping).

Content: This parameter is added when you want to track specific pieces of content. For example, if the content was a photograph of a girl wearing a green dress versus another picture where she is wearing a red dress. This can help identify specific content that appears to be a more significant driver of engagement (e.g., the picture of the red dress generated more sales than the picture of the green dress).

When tracking the success of influencer campaigns, four of the five parameters are commonly used: source, medium, campaign, and content. The terms parameter is used when you have paid for keywords.

The following is an example of a unique URL for paid influencer *"Jane D"* promoting a *"red dress"* on *"Instagram"* for the *"Gap."* The first part of the URL is a link to the item on the Gap website. The remainder of the URL contains the UTM parameters. These parameters have been bolded to make it easy for you to identify them.

Full URL: www.gap.com/ladiesreddress?utm_source=**instagram**&utm_medium=**paidinstagram**&utm_campaign=**janeD**&utm_content=**reddress**

This URL can then be embedded in an image. When the consumer clicks on the link, it will take them directly to the item on Gap's website.

If the social post includes words but not an image, the UTM parameter can be reduced in length using a URL shortener (e.g., bitly.com) and added as text.

Shortened URL (using bitly.com): https://bit.ly/3c26wBY

UTM parameters can be generated using the parameter creator in your analytics platform (e.g., Google Analytics). Alternatively, you can use a web-based parameter generator like UTM Tag Builder (www.utmtagbuilder.com).

Another common strategy for measuring success is to provide each influencer with a unique coupon code to add to their post and track the number of times the coupon is applied (e.g., JaneD20% or JoeB20%).

Internal Influencers

C-Suite

Senior executives can be powerful influencers. People form connections with other people more than companies or brand logos. Your audiences are more likely to follow and engage with a social media post from a person than they are a brand (Williams 2019). If written correctly, a social media post from a senior executive can feel more authentic and spontaneous and therefore more persuasive than a carefully created posting from the marketing department. Through consistent posting, senior executives can use social media to position themselves as thought leaders in their industry, adding credibility to and raising your company's profile. So, what type of content should they post, and on which platforms should it appear? One of the challenges that executives and companies face is maintaining a constant stream of content to post. To ensure that the quality and quantity of content do not dissipate, you need to create a manageable posting schedule (e.g., one post a week) and identify a variety of content to post.

There are at least four content categories—company, industry, thought leadership, and lifestyle. Company information will include sharing your company vision, behind-the-scenes insights, project updates, and breaking news. Industry information requires the executive to keep up-to-date with current news in their sector and share that with others. It can be as simple as reposting a recent news article (with a comment added to personalize it) or writing a new post. Thought leadership will perhaps be the most potent piece of content. A thought leadership post is where your executives share their insights and thoughts on a particular issue. A well-written thought piece can garner engagement, attract more followers, and position the executive as an industry leader (Moss 2022). Lifestyle content can help humanize the company and make the executive appear more approachable. To identify the appropriate content to post, consider the personality traits of the people who follow you and what is likely to resonate with them. It might be content related to travel, books, new technology, or entertainment events. The purpose of lifestyle content is to build a connection with followers and emotional capital with employees (Lozano 2019).

Emotional capital is the feeling of goodwill toward the organization and its leadership. The executives' actions and how they communicate can create an attachment to and pride in the company. When employees feel that attachment, they are motivated to advocate for the company (Huy and Shipilov 2012). Good examples of thought leaders include Richard Branson, founder, and CEO of Virgin Group. Branson actively engages with followers on LinkedIn, Twitter, and Instagram. On LinkedIn, Branson provides various content (photos, videos, status updates, and a blog) on his entrepreneurial efforts and the industries in which they operate (thought leadership, company, and industry). He ties his business activities to world events on Twitter and reposts lifestyle content (company and lifestyle). On Instagram, he shares photos and videos of his travels, famous friends, entertainment, and content related to his businesses (lifestyle, company). In some cases, he posts similar content on more than one platform. Still, the narrative is often calibrated to suit the characteristics of the platform and the audience (e.g., formal versus informal language or short posts on Twitter versus long posts on LinkedIn). Another example is entrepreneur and business magnate Elon Musk. Musk is an avid user of Twitter, where he often posts multiple times a day. His posts are free-flowing. It is not uncommon for him to fire off numerous posts in succession so that when strung together, they read like a conversation or story. His approach is very organic.

Employee Advocates

An employee advocate is a person who represents the interests of the company to internal and external audiences. Advocates help promote the business, products, services, and important news to others (Chen 2021). One research study examining employee advocacy revealed that over 70 percent of those surveyed indicated they are more likely to trust the content that everyday people share than companies. When an employee shares, brand messages can reach five times as many people as messages shared by official company accounts. In some instances, the lead to conversion is seven times greater when developed through an employee's social media (The Business Justification of Employee Advocacy 2020).

A company may already have a culture of advocacy whereby employees naturally share and promote company information via personal social channels. If this culture does not exist, it may be worthwhile to establish a program that will become part of the company culture over time (Mahato n.d.). There are five steps to creating a social media employee advocacy program.

Step 1: Create the Team

An employee advocacy program requires the support of several people. The team should comprise a program leader—someone who understands social media and has vision and leadership skills. You will also require one or more people from legal, IT, and marketing communications, a content creator, and someone to assist with the training of employees. Perhaps, most importantly, you will need one or more executive sponsors. The executive sponsor will become the face of the program. They must be strong supporters who are actively engaged in the company's social media efforts.

Step 2: Set Goals and KPIs

Once you have formed the team, the second step is to develop goals and key performance indicators (KPIs). Tie the program's goals to a specific company initiative, such as an important new product launch, a campaign, or an upcoming event. The goals that you set should be SMART: Specific, Measurable, Aggressive but Realistic, and Time-bound. For example, "increase the positive sentiment of X brand by 10 percent by the end of 2023 using LinkedIn and Facebook." A specific program goal will keep everyone focused on the desired outcome, time frame, and platforms. Once you have defined your goals, you need to determine how to measure success. There is no single metric that will determine the value of your program. Instead, the metric selected will be closely aligned with your goal. If the goal is to raise awareness of a new product, appropriate metrics will include reach and engagement. If the goal is to enhance reputation, then a relevant metric may be consumer sentiment. If the goal is to increase sales, the metric will be the number of products sold. The most commonly used metrics are reach, engagement, share of voice, sentiment, web traffic, lead generation, and sales.

Step 3: Recruit and Train

The third step is to recruit employees and build out the program. An effective employee advocate embodies the company's best interests and has been identified as a credible spokesperson because they are an expert, a long-term employee, or someone with influence. Look for employees with a genuine sense of company pride and affinity, value the opportunity to share their experiences, want to be recognized for their efforts, and are looking to enhance their reputation (Chen 2021). They also need to have a social media presence across relevant platforms, are actively engaged on those platforms, and whose current posting appears to generate engagement. Whereas the number of followers a person has is appropriate to use in selecting an advocate, it should not be the only criterion used. Quality of contacts and level of engagement are arguably more important, as is their motivation to be part of the program.

Once you have identified a handful of motivated employees, you need to empower and support them. Encourage them to use social media, seek their input, and listen to their suggestions. Support them by offering training, guidance on where and when to post, and a selection of approved resources and content to share. Remind them that there needs to be complete transparency in their postings. They will need to adhere to the FTC guidelines and disclose that they are an employee of the company. See Chapter 7 for guidance.

Step 4: Create Content

One of the reasons that employees agree to participate in an advocacy program is to help build their brand—enhance their reputation and position themselves as thought leaders. So, they will want high-quality content to share and some flexibility to select what to share. The employee advocacy team will need to create a selection of content for all the platforms that have been approved for use. Create a repository for this content and update it regularly. For each piece of information to be shared, offer variations in style and format. The employee needs to select the content that seems most authentic to them and that their followers will respond positively. Remember, quality is more important than quantity. If you only provide them with product information, enthusiasm for the program may wane. Provide a mixture of content, corporate, industry information, and lifestyle information that may interest their followers (Mahato n.d.). When deciding on which platforms to post on, think carefully about the intended audience and what type of content they would expect to find on that platform. Consumers utilize different social media platforms for various reasons.

Twitter

Consumers use Twitter for entertainment, to obtain discounts and deals, to hear breaking news, and to access exclusive content and information. So, Twitter is a great location to share the "hot off the press" news. Compared with Facebook, LinkedIn, and Pinterest, Twitter generates the smallest amount of sharing (Delzio 2015). To encourage engagement and social sharing, consider joining multiple tweets together to tell a story, a popular strategy by journalists reporting live events. Each Tweet provides a new piece of important information, and when the Tweets are read in succession, the whole story unfolds, and the message comes across as more conversational. A string of related tweets is considered a "thread" and is often denoted by a spool of thread emoji and numbered tweets (e.g., 1/, 2/). As mentioned early, Elon Musk uses this approach.

Engagement is linked to enjoyment. The more a follower enjoys your tweet, the more likely he is to engage (e.g., click on the link contained) and the higher level of engagement (e.g., moves from *watching* to *sharing* to *commenting*). Avoid excess company or product information (Kwon and Sung 2011). A tweet in a natural conversational tone is better than a perfectly crafted sound bite.

LinkedIn

LinkedIn is the ideal platform for allowing existing and potential customers, vendors, investors, and shareholders to learn about your company and products. This platform is perfect for sharing industry information, company updates, and thought leadership pieces. LinkedIn provides the opportunity to link to existing company materials, including blogs, interviews, videos, and white papers. Your company's materials will probably need to be redesigned to make them more palatable—less advertising, more educational.

Facebook

If LinkedIn is the business/corporate platform, Facebook is the personal platform. Facebook provides the opportunity to humanize the company and communicate its mission. Facebook is an excellent platform for reaching and interacting with potential decision makers and influencers less formally. This is the platform that you will use to share lifestyle content. Any content that follows into the other categories (company, industry, or thought leadership) should be redesigned to be less corporate.

Instagram

Consumers follow brands on Instagram because they love the brand. They are drawn to images and videos to learn about new products to purchase and help pass the time (Mander 2016). Visuals are compelling at evoking emotion and motivating social media users to react. Instagram is an excellent place to share behind the scene images of your business or lifestyle content. But not all pictures are share-worthy. Many photos end up on the cutting room floor or the digital trashcan. Just because Instagram offers you seemingly, unlimited storage doesn't mean that you should post everything. Be selective. When selecting photos to post, ask yourself, "is this image Instagram-worthy?" Or perhaps an even better question to ask yourself "is it billboard worthy?" If you are not willing to use the image in a billboard campaign then why would you use it on Instagram? In that case, this should help you identify high-quality images that evoke emotion and, therefore, encourage engagement (likes, comments, and sharing).

Blogs

Long-form blogs continue to be a popular method for sharing detailed updates, discussing industry events, and promoting thought leadership. The blog can be hosted on a third-party platform (e.g., blogger) or on your company website and shared (via URL) with your followers through any one of your social platforms. To ensure your blog is successful, write about a topic that will resonate with your audience and one that you know well—a subject you could easily and comfortably talk about in a meeting. Begin with a clear and concise idea—what is the blog's purpose, and what points do you want to get across? Write like you talk and allow your personality to shine through. When making statements, back them up with examples or data. When drawing from others' ideas, cite, and if appropriate, tag them so that they will see the blog (and hopefully share it with their network). Pose questions to encourage engagement. As for the length, shorter blogs (under 600 words) are often best for discussion and attention because the message is often straightforward, and the blog can be quickly read. But the short length can also be limiting in that it may lack sufficient substance to motivate readers to share the post on their social channels. A word count in the range of 600 to 1,500 may be more successful at getting your point across and encouraging sharing (White 2021). But remember, again, think about quality over quantity.

Step 5: Launch and Build Out the Program

Once you have your employees recruited and trained, you need to launch and build out the four program phases:

Phase 1: Consider this the orientation and learning phase. Spend the first month getting your employees comfortable with the various platforms and your expectations. Work alongside them to experiment with posting content and measuring results. It may be good to start with less promotional content and more community-building, employee pride, and industry information. Next, gradually introduce the promotional content. Observe what content resonates well with their audience and modify posting guidelines (platforms, type of content, timing, frequency) based on the results. Remind employees of any relevant industry guidelines they will need to adhere to. See Chapter 7 for guidance.

Phase 2: In this phase, you are empowering employees to share content on their own based on what they learned from phase 1. Ensure the company guidelines are clear about the frequency of posting, the type of content to post, and required disclosures. It may be necessary to send reminders (e.g., weekly) as employees may get sidetracked by other work responsibilities. Offer a small incentive and offer tokens of appreciation. Continue to measure success and modify guidelines.

Phase 3: Now may be the time to recruit more employees for the initiative. Measure and share the program's impact with senior executives and the broader workforce to build interest. Involve existing advocates in helping to identify and support new members.

Phase 4: This is when you review the goals you set, measure results to date, and adjust as needed. For example, if your goal was to increase positive sentiment by 10 percent by the end of 2023, you would not wait until December 31, 2023, to measure your results. Instead, you should measure at regular shorter intervals (weekly, bi-weekly, or monthly based on the posting guidelines you set for employees). If the results are not trending in the right direction and it appears that you will not meet your target, then regroup and revise. Offer refresher training to those employees who may need it. Continue to recognize and reward success.

An example of a company that touts the value of their employee advocacy program is the tech company Dell. More than 10,000 Dell employees worldwide use their social media to share company information. Dell reports that over 12 months, employee advocates generated more than 150,000 shares that yielded 45,000 clicks to Dell's website. In total, posts by employees reached an audience of over 1.2 million. Another example is the supply chain and logistics company Penske. Within the first quarter of the launch of their advocacy program, the company reported a 9,958 percent increase in total reach and a 333 percent increase in website click-throughs (How Dell Empowers It's Workforce On Social Media n.d.).

Consumer Influencers

This chapter has focused on the importance of social media influencers, executive thought leaders, and employee advocates. But we would be remiss if we didn't acknowledge that everyday consumers can also be helpful. Not all businesses need or can afford big names and famous faces. Small businesses may not have sufficient employees to develop a fully-fledged employee advocacy program. But what these businesses may have are loyal, happy, and socially savvy consumers to help spread the word online. Everyday consumers can organically post and should be encouraged to share. For example, a company can introduce a simple hashtag campaign that asks consumers to share a photo or provide a review on social media and include a recommended hashtag. Hashtag-related signage around the store and selfie stations all work to prompt a consumer to post.

Beyond the casual everyday consumer, there are also dedicated fans or brand advocates. Brand advocates are those people who organically infuse their favorite brand in their social media posts. The brand itself may be an extension of their identity (i.e., they mention the brand in their bio, social media profile image, or even have a brand tattoo). These fans delight in not only sharing information about their beloved brand but also recruiting others to join in the brand experience. Companies need to recognize and acknowledge the effort that these people put into these social media brand conversations. A simple "thumbs up" or a brief comment on their posting can motivate them to continue to share the good word. People like to be appreciated.

An old proverb says, "it takes a village to raise a child." The same adage applies to promoting a company's positive image on social media. To successfully utilize social media to get the word out about your business, you need the help and support of others. Recruiting external influencers may be appropriate for some companies. For others, it may be utilizing executives and employees or encouraging and acknowledging the work of everyday consumers and fans of your brand. Many social media users make light work.

References

Chen, J. November 01, 2021. "What Is Employee Advocacy and Does It Really Work?" https://sproutsocial.com/insights/what-is-employee-advocacy/.

Delzio, S. 2015. "Social Sharing Habits: New Research Reveals What People Like to Share : Social Media Examiner." *SocialMedia Examiner*. www.socialmediaexaminer.com/social-sharing-habits-new-research/.

"Different Types of Influencers: Mega, Macro, Micro and Nano." July 30, 2020. www.amire.com.au/blog/different-types-of-influencers-%EF%BB%BF%EF%BB%BFmega-macro-micro-nano%EF%BB%BF/.

Halverson Group. 2015. "IZEA'S 2015 State of Sponsored Social Study." www.slideshare.net/RonHalversonPhD/2015-state-of-sponsored-social-55896715.

"How Dell Empowers It's Workforce On Social Media." n.d. https://everyonesocial.com/wp-content/uploads/2018/06/How-Dell-Empowers-Its-Workforce-On-Social-Media.pdf (accessed March 26, 2022).

Huy, Q. and A. Shipilov. September 18, 2012. "The Key to Social Media Success Within Organizations." *MIT Sloan Review*. https://sloanreview.mit.edu/article/the-key-to-social-media-success-within-organizations/#:~:text=Our%20earlier%20research%20on%20organizational,%2C%20pride%2C%20attachment%20and%20fun.

Influencer Marketing Hub. 2021. "The State of Influencer Marketing 2021: Benchmark Report." https://influencermarketinghub.com/influencer-marketing-benchmark-report-2021/.

Kwon, E.S. and Y. Sung. 2011. "Follow Me ! Global Marketers' Twitter Use." *Journal of Interactive Advertising* 12, no. 1, pp. 4–16. https://doi.org/10.1080/15252019.2011.10722187.

Lozano, D. October 25, 2019. "Social Media Strategies for the C-Suite and Senior Management That Actually Work." www.socialmediatoday.com/news/social-media-strategies-for-the-c-suite-and-senior-management-that-actually/565823/.

Mahato, L. n.d. "Empower Your Workforce With Employee Advocacy." *Hootsuite*. www.hootsuite.com/webinars/empower-your-workforce-with-employee-advocacy (accessed March 26, 2022).

Mander, J. 2016. "Half of Instagrammers Follow Brands." *Globalwebindex*. www.globalwebindex.net/blog/half-of-instagrammers-follow-brands.

Maoz, Y. 2016a. *First Steps for Healthy Influencer Relationships*. Klear Blog.

Maoz, Y. 2016b. *Marketing Brief Template for an Influencer Campaign*. Klear Blog.

Moss, L. 2022. "Executives on Social Media: The Value of Social Media." https://everyonesocial.com/blog/executives-on-social-media/.

Rahal, A. 2020. "Is Influencer Marketing Worth It in 2020?" *Forbes*. www.forbes.com/sites/theyec/2020/01/10/is-influencer-marketing-worth-it-in-2020/?sh=44417a3d31c5.

Single Grain. 2021. "Influencer Marketing Strategy: The Ultimate Guide to Growing Your Business With Brand Partnerships." www.singlegrain.com/content-marketing-strategy-2/guide-influencer-marketing/.

The Business Justification of Employee Advocacy. 2020. https://everyonesocial.com/resources/business-justification-employee-advocacy/.

White, C. December 01, 2021. "What Is the Ideal Length for a Blog Post in 2022?" www.bramework.com/ideal-blog-post-length/.

Williams, R. April 18, 2019. "Social Media Users Trust Fellow Consumers More Than Brands." www.marketingdive.com/news/social-media-users-trust-fellow-consumers-more-than-brands-study-finds/552994/.

CHAPTER 6

The Power of Persuasion

Do you remember the famous line from the 1989 movie *Field of Dreams*, starring Kevin Costner? "If you build it, he will come." Many companies have, in the past, and some continue to do so today, assume that social media is a field of dreams—build a social presence and consumers will connect with your company. Unfortunately, that is not the case. Simply having a social presence is not enough. To have overall success in social media and encourage social word of mouth (sWOM), your company needs to apply the powers of persuasion.

One of the best-known and respected scholars on the topic of persuasion, Dr. Robert Cialdini, offers six principles of social influence that can also be applied to social media. Dr. Cialdini, by observing the persuasion tactics of influential people (i.e., religious leaders, salespeople, telemarketers, and so on), followed by experimental studies, developed the persuasion principles of reciprocity, scarcity, authority, consistency, likeability, and consensus. Cialdini outlines these in his book, *Influence: The Psychology of Persuasion*, and more recently, *Yes: 50 Scientifically Proven Ways to Be Persuasive*. Both are great reads. How do we apply these principles to social media communication?

Reciprocity

The principle of reciprocity is the idea that people feel obligated to give back when they receive something. And, all of us have felt the influential power of the need to reciprocate. Did you ever get a birthday present from someone and then felt required to return the favor when it was their big day (even if you had not originally planned on it)? Have you made sure you returned a dinner invite after being guests at your friend's home?

There are also numerous examples of how this principle has been applied in commercial settings. Most commonly, it can be seen in business gift giving (e.g., holiday card or gift from a company). It also might be as small as a coupon, calendar, or magnet. A common fundraising tactic that many charities use is giving potential donors personalized address label stickers in their donation request mailing. The idea, of course, is that you if you receive (and use) this gift, you will feel obligated to donate. The impact of this principle is enhanced when the gift is unexpected, personalized, and it ideally should happen *before* you ask them to provide personal information, share the information with others, or make a purchase (Cialdini 2006).

The practice of reciprocity is alive and well in the online arena. Take, for example, Dropbox that offers free storage if you share details of your adoption of the service with friends. Another common practice for companies and bloggers alike is to provide great content via posts, white papers, webinars, and sometimes, e-books in the hopes that you will provide them with your e-mail address. Offering digital free samples, such as the first chapter of an e-book, is another great way to increase the likelihood of a reader purchasing the entire book. So, how can this principle relate to social media? First, social media can be used as the method of distributing great content. Mailchimp, a marketing automation company, embraces both LinkedIn and Instagram to share customer profiles and ideas of how to navigate business life during COVID-19. They not only reinforced their brand but also educated small businesses on how to engage remote employees (Morrison 2021). Another approach is to provide a small favor or acknowledge the value of your consumers or followers. For example, retweeting or sharing an individual's posts makes them more likely to return the retweet or share. Commenting, liking, @mentions, and tagging are also forms of acknowledgment that may increase your likelihood of having consumers not only engage with your brand but share your content. As further evidence that social media provides a venue for two-way conversions, consumers can now easily "reward" accounts. Twitter offers a tipping feature located on the account's profile and TikTok allows creators to receive purchased virtual gifts from viewers that they can later exchange for money. While there are a host of motivating factors to give, many users do it because they want the reciprocal, "Shout out!" on the account.

Reciprocity is also at the heart of what has been called "surprise and delight" marketing campaigns. In essence, marketers are connecting with consumers often via social media (or at least finding them when on social monitoring platforms) and providing them with surprise gifts (birthday, holiday, or "just because"), personalized product samples, coupons, or reward discounts. This element of surprise, some would argue, is one of the most powerful marketing tools. It can be addictive, drive behavior change, improve brand perceptions, and magnify emotions. It can also add some needed excitement into not only a personal but also a commercial relationship (Redick 2013; Harris 2015). It can be used to reward loyal consumers and "re-engage" consumers that have become rather dormant online (CrowdTwist 2015).

Surprise and delight campaigns can be very effective strategies that are relatively inexpensive. Take, for instance, Kleenex's Feel Good campaign. During winter, Kleenex found 50 consumers in Israel who were discussing their illness on Facebook. They prepared a personalized Kleenex Kit, contacted connected Facebook friends to get a physical address, and sent the package to the ill individuals via a courier within 1 to 2 hours of the post. Every person who got a kit posted a photo with a positive message on their Facebook wall. The result was over-650,000 impressions and 1,800 interactions (Shaprio 2012). While this had an incredible response rate, getting consumers to share their surprise on social media is not that uncommon (CrowdTwist 2015). One Canadian survey found that women were more likely than men to tell family and friends about a surprise and delight experience (Harris 2015).

Reciprocity commonly blurs the online and offline lines. To illustrate, Bud Light's #UpforWhatever campaign, which culminated in the creation of a fictional city called Whatever, USA (aka Crested Butte, Colorado), became a "content factory" for social media. One thousand consumers were selected out for 200,000 applicants for a weekend filled with random surprises, which included a faux beach, 80s pop star Vanilla Ice, and circus rides. Only 50 of the 37,000 pieces of content that were shared online were created by Bud Light; the rest were all consumer-created (Monllos 2015; Hughes 2014).

Authority

Authority or expert status is a classic method of persuasion used in marketing (Cialdini 2006). From an early age, we have been brought up to listen, respect, and be obedient to those in authority. Therefore, it is not surprising that this principle also works in relationship to making consumption choices. Consumers will often turn to experts, especially if they are not sure about a consumption decision. The idea being—they know better than me. Marketers have long been aware of the importance of communicating authority in marketing material using both explicit and symbolic means in establishing it. Think back to TV commercials that contain a lawyer (or actor) seated at his or her desk surrounded by framed diplomas and leather-bound books, or cliche advertising statements like "9 out of 10 doctors recommended [insert product here]." Forewords on books written by experts, a high consumer report rating, and product ownership by a fashionable, well-photographed celebrity are some of the countless examples of how you can convey authority in a consumer culture.

Online, the same principles apply. Amazon highlights positive comments from well-known experts in the book description. Bloggers will often state on their website (using appropriate media logos) newspapers, magazine, and TV shows where they have been featured. Website URL addresses that end in .edu or .gov or also examples of how authority can be quickly and succinctly conveyed online.

Within the cluttered, muddied waters of social media, we could argue that authority and credibility matters even more, and social media platforms have also realized its importance. The most popular social media platforms have devised quick, a visual shorthand to indicate whether an account is "officially" from a celebrity or business. Social media platforms have created verification symbols, often in the form of a checkmark located next to a user's profile information. There are also additional cues to indicate legitimacy—the year that the account opened, location, dedicated #hashtag campaign, and simply providing a coherent description void of spelling and grammar mistakes. Also, the careful selection of cover and profile photos, the use of logos, the selection of keywords, and the reporting of accomplishments in your bio or company description can all help convey authority. Beyond account and platform structure, authority is predominately established by an account's content. In the end, success on social media and #sharing comes down to good content. Are you providing consistent, high-quality, and deep knowledge on specific topics?

Scarcity

If you spend a few minutes watching the Home Shopping Network (HSN) or QVC (Quality, Value, Convenience), you have seen the scarcity principle in action. Both of these networks include a countdown clock of just how many items and time is left to purchase this shiny, new product that will certainly make your life better. McDonald's owes the success of the McRib and Shamrock Shake to the limited time they are listed on the menu. Yes, there is something extra appealing about a product that seems to be going away in the very near future or is only offered to a "select" group of people.

An increasing number of e-commerce websites are also putting this principle into practice. Consider the value-travel website Expedia. After searching for a hotel, you are not only notified of the price but also (in red font) told how many rooms are left at this rate. To further punctuate the scarcity principle, the site includes a "Daily Deal" countdown clock, which lets you know how little time you have left to grab this great deal. The site also tells you just how many others are looking at this deal to entice you further into a purchase. In general, e-commerce stores are doing a better job of indicating how close an item is to being sold out. Scarcity has also been used to launch new services online. In 2004, Gmail began solely through invitations—you could only have an account if someone invited you. Scarcity has also been used in a similar way to launch a new social media platform. This strategy worked for Facebook who at first restricted account membership to Harvard students, before slowly allowing other universities and high schools to join, by which time the rest of us all were eager to have our account. One could also argue the success of the Stories feature has largely to do with the limited viewing time of their photos. Arguably, social media best utilizes the scarcity principle by distributing messages that incorporate access to content for a limited time, offering discount coupons and exclusive deals for a "select" consumer group, short-duration contests (e.g., best photo with product +Halloween theme posted by the end of today), and limit product supplies.

Commitment and Consistency

Consumers are generally committed to engaging in future behavior that is consistent with their prior behavior (Cialdini 2006). For example, if a consumer has supported a company in the past, they are more likely to support it in the future. If a consumer likes your post on Facebook, then there is a good chance that he would be willing to share that post with his social network. Sometimes, the consumer just needs to be asked. Think about the number of times you have been asked to make a commitment—"please like," "please retweet," "download," "subscribe here." The key for marketers is to get a consumer to make a small commitment, often referred to as the *foot-in-the-door* technique, which in time may lead to a larger commitment such as a recommendation or purchase. Commitment can begin with the consumer following your page, followed by liking a post, providing a comment, sharing the post with his network, talking about the brand, and recommending the company or brand to others. This commitment needs to be acknowledged by the company. For instance, when a consumer follows your company Twitter account, respond with a "Thanks @carriemunoz for following, be sure to check out our xxx." In acknowledging the act, you are also reminding the consumer of their commitment. It is highly unlikely that all your consumers will instantly make the leap from following your page to writing long, detailed recommendations. So, you need to help move your consumers through this commitment process by developing social strategies that encourage consumers to follow, like, share, comment, and so on. One popular strategy is to introduce a competition that encourages consumers to engage with the brand and to help spread positive sWOM.

In 2021, Goldfish crackers created a duet challenge for TikTok titled, #GoForTheHandful. Consumers (and presumably big Goldfish fans) were asked to create a TikTok video where they were trying to hold more Goldfish crackers in their hand than 7'4 pro basketball player Boban Marjanovic (he can hold 301). The campaign received over 12 billion views on TikTok (TikTok 2022). Another strategy that communicates commitment is to provide consumers with meaningful and interesting information and make it easy to share. To illustrate, Spotify embraces the use of personalized, sharable data through their "Year in Review." Each year users receive and share via social media "Spotify Wrapped" share cards which contain a music and podcast overview that includes data on an individual's favorite songs, artists, minutes listened to, and much more. To increase the likelihood of sharing, Spotify offers Story Lenses

(Kaleidoscope and Data Story Quiz), the ability to customize share cards and social media integration with Instagram, Facebook, Twitter, Snapchat, and TikTok (Miller 2020). Spotify Wrapped has been wildly successful. In 2020, there were 60 million shares of Spotify Wrapped. This number is made more amazing given that they had 90 million users! (Shalvoy 2021).

Social Proof

The persuasion principle of social proof comes down to judging something on the actions of others (Cialdini 2006). If others like it, it must be good! We often refer to this as consensus. For example, would you rather go to an empty restaurant or one with a line out the door? Would you feel more comfortable purchasing a bestseller or a book with only 120 reviews? Social proof is perhaps the most frequently used persuasion principle online and within social media. There are numerous ways to communicate social proof. E-commerce website Zulily and others are quick to point out which products sell well—adding a "popular" icon over specific product images, along with how many of these products have just been sold directly under the price. Other retail websites also provide ample opportunities for consumers to read product reviews, which can dramatically impact whether a consumer purchases a product. Product reviews have also evolved well beyond textual descriptions and now included uploaded images and videos, which only enhance their level of influence (e.g., Remember Rent the Runway from Chapter 1). Outside of product reviews, simple consumer testimonial delivered on a landing page and via social media also serves as powerful examples of social proof.

Social media metrics are not only important for marketers but consumers are a form of social proof. Consumers will look at available metrics (e.g., likes, shares, retweets) to determine a message's (and the messenger's) worth. Consumers are more likely to value and share information gleaned from an account with an abundance of followers than they are for accounts that fail to attract the interest of consumers. The same is true with a post that has been liked, shared, retweeted, and favorited hundreds of times. Given that we see these posts from people whom we know and like amplifies the effect, making us more likely to share.

Liking

There is a reason that we tend to follow the advice of our friends, family, and the occasional celebrity—it is because we like them (well, most of the time). Not only do we listen to what they say, but we often do what they ask. The secret to success in word-of-mouth (WOM) marketing is to be likable. So, how can a company get consumers to like them on social media? Success begins at the source of the message, followed by the content of the message. Given that Chapter 4 discussed at length the content of your message, we will focus our discussion here on the source of the message.

If you are fortunate enough to have someone within your company who is well liked by your consumers, then it may be helpful to have him or her contribute to your social media. Take, for example, Richard Branson, founder of the Virgin Group. When posting to his personal social media accounts, he frequently tags a Virgin company account. The account then retweets or shares the posting with its followers. Branson's Facebook, LinkedIn, and Twitter posts attract hundreds of comments and thousands of shares. In the advertising world, they would say that Branson has social value. His social value originates from his personality and social status. Another factor that also contributes to his social value is his credibility, perceived expertise, objectivity, and trustworthiness. When a communication source has high social value, this can result in a halo effect. A halo effect is a cognitive bias in which the overall positive impression that we have of one person can transfer to another person, product, or unrelated item (Solomon 2017). So, when Branson mentions or recommends a product, service, idea, or another person on social media, the positive feelings that a consumer has about Branson may transfer to the item or person mentioned. But, what if your company does not have a Richard Branson (and let's be honest most companies do not), how do you get consumers to like your brand? Having a famous person posting on your social media can be helpful, but it is not always necessary. Everyday consumers can be just as influential. Have you ever noticed a posting in your Facebook newsfeed that said that one of your friends liked a specific brand? Have you found yourself retweeting or sharing something that a good friend or colleague posted, even if you were not all that familiar with the item or topic they mentioned? If so, the chances are that the person who posted the item is a good friend, someone, who in your eyes, has social value. In Chapter 2, we discussed the power of social consumers, everyday people who have the ability to reach and influence a large number of consumers. In Chapter 5, we examined how companies are using these social influencers to spread positive sWOM. It may be appropriate for your company to solicit the help of influencers to mention your company on social media or to contribute guest posts. We also discussed how your network of followers could be helpful. Each of your followers on social media has the power and potential to introduce your company to a new group of consumers. Tourism Australia offers a great example of how everyday consumers can be influential in spreading sWOM.

Social Sharing at Tourism Australia

Tourism Australia is an Australian government agency founded in 2004, charged with developing strategies to promote Australia as a destination for leisure and business travel. The agency has a website, LinkedIn profile, and Twitter account under the name Tourism Australia (www.tourism.australia.com) and a website, Facebook, Twitter, Instagram, and YouTube account under the name Australia (www.australia.com). Tourism Australia recognized that, perhaps, their greatest asset in spreading the word about Australia was not their social media team of three, but their then 4 million plus Facebook fans, 23 million residents, and 6 million international visitors (Jafri 2013). To encourage sWOM, the agency decided to try something that many companies and organizations would shy away from—they turned their Facebook page over to their fans. Fans and followers were responsible for deciding what they wanted to see on Facebook, were allowed to submit items for sharing, and were empowered to respond to questions posted online. The process began by inviting fans and followers to submit personal photographs of Australia. Fans posted these photographs using a photo-board app and with the understanding that their photographs may be used for promotional purposes. Over 1,000 photographs showcasing iconic landmarks, flora, and fauna, and natural scenic beauty were submitted each day and shared on Facebook and Instagram. Whereas many of these photographs showed current-day

Australia, some dated back as far as 1910. Each week approximately 35 of the photographs were chosen by the Tourism Australia social media team to be published in a digital album—Friday Fan Photos. Every image chosen was designed to tell a story and allow for a story to be told (Tourism Australia 2013). When a picture was posted, other fans would add comments, provide additional details, and add their perspective to create a rich narrative of life in Australia. Fans were even allowed to add their family photos to the timeline. These photographs promoted a series of discussions on traditions and vacations particularly among family and friends who may not, at least at that time, have been a follower of the Tourism Australia page. This approach allowed Tourism Australia to extend its reach in a more personal less promotional manner. Fans, whose photographs were posted, became experts, actively engaging with other fans and responding to questions about their photographs. Fans were even asked to recommend captions for individual photographs. Many of these consumer-generated photos attracted thousands of likes, shares, and comments. After turning their social media over to their fans, Tourism Australia's Facebook page became the most liked page in Australia and the most-popular destination page in the world (Jafri 2013).

So, how do social influence and persuasion apply to this example?

Reciprocity

Tourism Australia posted consumer photographs to the agency's social media account. They hand-selected a small number each week to be published in a digital album. This act alone communicates to consumers that the agency has seen and valued their contribution, which is likely to motivate consumers to continue to participate.

Authority

There is no one more qualified to talk about what it is like to live in Australia than their residents, and no one is more qualified to talk about how wonderful a place it is to visit than tourists. It is easy for social media accounts like Tourism Australia's to become just another marketing channel, with professional photographs accompanied by carefully crafted advertising. But, as we know, social media is about communicating. So, by turning the account over to their fans and followers who are the real experts, the account loses that promotional feel, and in its place, something more authentic emerges. Personal photographs and stories from real people help to increase the persuasiveness of the message, particularly when they are shared by someone you know.

Commitment and Consistency

If you posted a photograph on Tourism Australia's Facebook page and that photograph generated likes, comments, and questions, would you feel compelled to jump in, engage with these other consumers, and answer their questions? If your photograph was one of the 35 selected for Fan Photo Fridays, would you want to share that with your social network? When Tourism Australia empowered its fans to answer questions, they were encouraging them to continue to engage with the page.

Social Proof

The more likes, comments, and shares that a posting receives, the more likely it is to appear in a consumer's newsfeed and the potential for greater engagement. We tend to "like" what our network of friends and family like. When this social proof originates from those whom we love, like, admire or respect, the posting has personal relevance and we are motivated to engage.

Liking

We have no doubt that celebrities like actors Hugh Jackman and Chris Hemsworth are great ambassadors for Australia and that consumers will watch their Tourism Australia commercials on YouTube and Facebook. Indeed, famous faces that we admire and respect are highly successful at capturing our attention. However, beyond the initial "like," we are unlikely to engage any further, and therefore, the persuasiveness of the message is limited. But, when your BBF, brother, second cousin twice removed, or friend from kindergarten posts a picture that resonates with you and tells a familiar story, a story that you can and want to contribute to it has more influence. It may be a current photograph or one from yesteryear that evokes feelings of nostalgia. Either way, your desire to engage with it is greater, and because of this, it is likely that you will move beyond simply liking the photo to commenting (perhaps repeatedly) and sharing the image with others by either tagging them in your comment or hitting the "Share" button.

So, what can you learn from Tourism Australia that you can apply to your company?

- Let your consumers guide the type of content you post on social media. Ask them what they want to see.
- In some cases, it is your consumers who are the experts, not your employees. Empower your consumers to be the authority figure.
- Consumer-generated content is a great way of sourcing fresh material to share on social media.
- Consumer-generated content may be perceived as more authentic, and therefore, may generate higher levels of engagement. Higher engagement can lead to increased visibility.
- Consumer-generated content can help generate sWOM with your existing fan base. It also helps you extend your reach beyond your network and attract new followers.
- Always acknowledge the commitment of your consumers. Thank them for their contribution and effort. Engage them in conversation. This will encourage them to continue to engage with your account.
- Every picture you share on social media should tell a story and allow for a story to be told.
- Allow your consumers to help you tell the story.

References

Cialdini, R. 2006. *Influence: The Psychology of Persuasion.* New York, NY: Harper Business.

CrowdTwist. 2015. *How Surprise and Delight Amplifies Loyalty Marketing Strategies.* Retrieved from https://loyalty360.org/Loyalty360/media/ResearchAndReportDocs/Surprise_Whitepaper_020415_online_(3).pdf.

Harris, R. December 2015. "Why Brand Should 'Surprise and Delight' Customers (Survey)." *Marketing*.

Hughes, T. September 2014. "Bud Light Turns Tiny Ski Town Into Whatever, USA." *USA Today*.

Jafri, S. 2013. "9 Content Marketing Lessons From Tourism Australia | Search Engine Watch." *Search Engine Watch*. doi:2016-08-11.

Miller, C. 2020. "Spotify Wrapped 2020: How to Find Your Top Songs, Artists, Albums, and More." 9TO5Mac. Retrieved from https://9to5mac.com/2020/12/09/how-to-spotify-wrapped-2020/.

Monllos, K. June 2015. "Whatever, USA: Bud Light's Party Town as 'Content Factory.'" *Adweek*.

Morrison, C. 2021. "9 B2B Social Media Examples to Inspire Your Strategy." Everyone Social. Retrieved from https://everyonesocial.com/blog/b2b-social-media-examples/.

Redick, S. May 2013. "Surprise Is Still the Most Powerful Marketing Tool." Harvard Business Review.

Shalvoy, J. 2021. "Spotify Unwrapped: Inside the Company's Biggest Marketing Campaign." *Variety*. Retrieved from https://variety.com/2021/music/news/spotify-wrapped-marketing-shares-1235139981/.

Shaprio, L. April 2012. "Social Media Campaigns That Achieve the Unthinkable: 100% Response Rates." *The Jerusalem Post*.

Solomon, M.R. 2017. *Consumer Behavior: Buying Having, and Being*, 12th ed. Hoboken, NJ: Pearson.

TikTok. 2022. "#GoForTheHandful." Retrieved from www.tiktok.com/tag/GoForTheHandful.

Tourism Australia. 2013. "The World's Biggest Social Media Team." Retrieved from www.slideshare.net/TourismAustralia/the-worlds-biggest-social-media-team-16545786.

CHAPTER 7

Legal and Regulatory Issues

Singer and songwriter Rihanna tweeted "Listening to ANTI" to her more than 55 million fans. Included with the tweet was a photo of Rihanna wearing Dolce and Gabbana gold jewel-encrusted headphones. The image was retweeted over 175,000 times and received over 284,000 likes. The headphones, which retailed for $9,000, sold out within 24 hours (Wouk 2016). On December 12, 2016, model Hailey Baldwin shared with her 10+ million Instagram followers a photo of her and four famous friends relaxing on a yacht with the message, "work is tough." The image was part of a promotional campaign for the infamous Fyre Festival—a music festival to be hosted in the Bahamas (Allan and Wood 2020). On the same day, in a collaborative endeavor, approximately 60 celebrity models and influencers posted an orange firelike square to their personal Instagram pages, effectively flooding social media channels (Karp 2017). Bella Hadid's orange square Instagram post (12.8 million followers) was accompanied by the message "CAN'T wait for #fyrefestival," a series of emoticons, and a link to the Fyre Festival website. Festival organizers report that this combined effort generated over 300 million social media impressions within a couple of days (Abadi 2019).

Engaging celebrities in sharing positive word of mouth (WOM) with their legions of fans is a popular strategy offline and now online. Marketers are knocking on the virtual doors of A-, B-, C-, and even D-list celebrities to solicit their help in spreading positive WOM. One can only imagine the jubilation in the marketing department of Dolce and Gabbana after the success of Rihanna's tweet. Equally excited were the organizers of the Fyre Festival.

Celebrity support for a brand can be priceless. It can not only increase brand exposure, but it may also increase sales. However, their support is not always free. In fact, celebrity endorsement often comes with a hefty price tag. Celebrities understand the potential influence they have over fans and they expect to *be handsomely compensated*. The cost of employing a celebrity to share positive social WOM (sWOM) varies based on their social status and their number of followers. Some celebrities charge as little as $1,000 a tweet, but big names demand and receive more. A post from MMA fighter Conor McGregor costs $169,000. If you can afford a little more, you may want to consider entrepreneur and reality TV star Khloe Kardashian, who commands $598,000 for a single post. Popstar and actor Selena Gomez will often only commit to one sponsored Instagram post per month. But that post could set you back $886,000 (Olya 2021). But what are small-to-medium-size businesses with limited marketing budgets to do? How can they spread positive sWOM?

The answer lies, at least in part, in their ability to harness the influence of noncelebrity influencers (see Chapter 5) and everyday social media users including employees. However, companies face a fine line between encouraging influencers and consumers to share positive sWOM and incentivizing them. And, if that line is crossed, you may find yourself in some legal hot water. This chapter will examine the Federal Trade Commission's (FTC's) Endorsement Guidelines and what they mean for marketers who want to embrace and encourage sWOM. We will also discuss the importance of and process of creating a social media policy.

Social Influencer Examples

The best way to begin our discussion on legal and regulatory issues is to offer some examples, each of which highlights a different way in which everyday consumers and social influencers can help spread positive information about brands:

> **Teami:** Teami, the maker of detox teas, paid entertainers Cardi B, Jordin Sparks, and eight other influencers to endorse its product on Instagram. Each influencer posted a picture of themselves holding the product, accompanied by text boasting how the product helped them get back in shape, improved their energy levels, or enhanced their skin (Williams 2020).
>
> **Lord & Taylor:** U.S. department store Lord & Taylor hired 50 fashion bloggers to take pictures of themselves wearing a paisley print

dress and post them to Instagram. Each photo was captioned with positive statements (e.g., so excited to be dressing for spring in this dress from @lordandtaylor's new #DesignLab collection!).

Sour Patch Kids: Mondelez International, a leading manufacturer of candy, enlisted the help of social media influencer, Logan Paul, to help promote Sour Patch Kids. The goal of the campaign was to increase awareness of the candy brand among the core market—teens. Once a day for one week, Paul posted a Snapchat story that incorporated the popular candy.

Despite the appeal of these sWOM strategies, each of them suffers from a similar legal problem. To the average social media user, these social media messages (tweets, pins, posts) may appear organic—independent evaluations or support for a product or brand. However, these messages were not created and posted independently. Each of these was a planned marketing promotion, in which the brand or appointed agency incentivized social influencers to engage in sWOM. In other words, a material connection existed between the individual who posted the message and the company, and this relationship was not disclosed to the public. In orchestrating and sharing these posts on social media, the brand and the participating social media users failed to adhere to FTC's Endorsement Guidelines. Under Act 5 of FTC's Endorsement Guidelines, these social messages are misleading and potentially deceptive. Such practices can lead to enforcement action by the FTC and substantial fines. So, who is the FTC, what is the extent of their power, how do they determine of if an action is deceptive, and what are the guidelines that you need to follow?

The FTC and Social Media

The FTC is a bipartisan federal agency with the broad responsibility of promoting competition while protecting consumers from acts and practices that may cause them harm. One practice that the FTC monitors is deceptive advertising (Federal Trade Commission 2016a). Here, the FTC's duty is to enforce truth-in-advertising laws—federal laws that say advertising "must be truthful, not misleading, and when appropriate, backed by scientific research" (Federal Trade Commission 2016b).

An analysis of deception first begins with determining whether a representation, omission, or practice is *likely to mislead* the consumer. Most deception involves written or oral misrepresentations, or omissions of material information, such as failure to disclose a material connection between an endorser and a brand. The FTC need not determine that consumers are misled to conclude that an act or practice is deceptive (Burkhalter, Wood, and Tryce 2014). The key is "likely to mislead." The second element is that the representation, omission, or practice must be likely to mislead *reasonable consumers under the circumstances*. The FTC will evaluate the entire advertisement or transaction, to decide how a reasonable consumer is likely to respond (Dingle 1983). The FTC holds that "reasonable consumers may be less skeptical of personal opinion (i.e., endorsements) than of advertising claims" (Petty and Andrews 2008, 12). Nonetheless, "reasonable consumer" is difficult to define and often leads to protracted litigation (Burkhalter, Wood, and Tryce 2014). The third element is materiality. A representation, omission, or practice must be a *material* one for deception to occur (*F.T.C v. Transnet Wireless Corp* 2007). A material representation, omission, or practice is the one that is likely to impact a consumer's decision-making related to a product (Burkhalter, Wood, and Tryce 2014).

In addition to enforcing these laws, the FTC also educates businesses on how to comply with the law. Educational resources are typically in the form of published guides. One of the guides published by the FTC specifically addresses the use of testimonials and endorsements in advertising. Before we go any further, we should note that the FTC uses the terms "endorsement" and "testimonials" interchangeably for the purpose of enforcing the FTC Act (Federal Trade Commission 2008). The FTC literature that references social media also utilizes the term "advocate" when referring to individuals who deliver endorsements through social media. To keep things simple from this point forward, we will use the term "endorsement" when referring to the act of voicing approval for a brand and "endorser" when referring to those social media users (consumers, social influencers, and celebrities) who are responsible for these social media posts.

The FTC's Guide to Testimonial and Endorsements was first published in 1975. The purpose of this guide was to ensure that advertising messages were clear and truthful. The growing use of social media for endorsements forced the FTC to revisit these guidelines, and in 2009, a substantially revised version of the guides was published. The need for revision was based on the fact that, on social media, it is difficult to determine whether a relationship exists between the individual posting the message and the brand they have mentioned. In traditional advertising (i.e., television, radio, print), the consumer can readily identify an endorsement message and the endorser's association with a particular brand. For example, when British actress Keira Knightley appears in a TV commercial or magazine advertisement for Chanel perfume, we understand that she is being paid to appear in these advertising messages. However, when this endorsement appears on social media, it is difficult for consumers to determine if the posting is consumer-generated earned media. In other words, it is difficult to tell if the message was posted by the endorser, independent of the brand, or if the endorser posted it in consideration for some form of payment. The endorsement confusion on social media can be attributed to an individual's personal account being used to send the message. When an endorsement is shared from a personal account, the typical consumer may not be aware that a relationship, referred to by the FTC as a "material connection," exists between the marketer and the person who posted the online message—the endorser. The ability to distinguish between an authentic uncompensated endorsement and a paid one may even be more difficult when the influencer is not a celebrity or, unbeknownst to the reader, an employee of the company.

When to Disclose—Material Connection

The key to determining if and when disclosure is required is the presence or absence of a material connection.

> Material connections may be defined as any connection between an advocate [endorser] and a marketer that could affect the credibility consumers give to that advocate's statements. Important examples of 'material connections' may include; (i) consideration

(benefits or incentives such as monetary compensation, loaner products, free products or services, in-kind gifts, special access privileges, affiliate commissions, discounts, gift cards, sweepstakes entries or nonmonetary incentives) provided by a marketer to an advocate, or (ii) a relationship between a marketer and an advocate (such as an employment relationship) (WOMMA 2012).

The following may help improve your understanding of what constitutes a material connection:

Imagine that you follow a fashion blog. In one blog post (e.g., tweet, status update, or blog entry), your favorite blogger writes a positive review of a particular item of clothing. You, the reader, may feel inclined to take this blogger's opinion into consideration when deciding to purchase the item. What if you were told that she was paid to discuss and endorse the item, would this alter how you view her recommendation? This incidence occurred with the Lord & Taylor example presented early in this chapter. The department store paid 50 bloggers between $1,000 and $4,000 to promote a particular paisley print dress. Bloggers posted a photograph of themselves wearing the dress on Instagram and other social media sites. These posts reached 11.4 million individual Instagram users over two days and amassed 328,000 brand engagements (Federal Trade Commission 2016c). The dress quickly sold out. A material connection existed between the marketer and the endorser in the form of monetary compensation (Beck 2015a). The social media users who were responsible for sharing sWOM failed to disclose their connection with the band they were endorsing.

In the Fyre Festival example, the event organizers compensated the models and social media influencers for their efforts, but none of them communicated this to their followers. Subsequently, a class action suit was filed against the organizers and 100 "Jane Does" (influencers) for negligent misrepresentation, fraud, breach of contract, and for failing to provide the promised experience (Sass 2017).

The FTC asserts that consumers have the right to know who is behind these sponsored messages, particularly if they could influence their purchase decisions (WOMMA 2014). According to the FTC, regardless of the type of message (e.g., visual or text), each of these sWOM messages was misleading and potentially deceptive.

When a Disclosure Is Not Required?

There are a few scenarios when a material connection does not exist, and therefore, disclosure is not required. The first is when a consumer mentions a product that he or she paid for himself or herself. If the consumer posts about an item he or she purchased and is not being compensated for that post, then a material connection, as defined by the FTC, does not exist (Federal Trade Commission 2013a).

Another instance when it is not necessary to disclose is when the posting is made from the brand's official account, as was the case with the Sour Patch Kids promotion. Logan Paul, who was recruited for the campaign, was a well-known social media influencer among teenagers. A material connection exists because Paul was financially compensated for his participation in the promotion. But, because Paul posted some of his Snapchat videos from the official Sour Patch Kids account, it is not necessary for him to disclose his material connection. Paul did, however, also post from his personal account. It is necessary to disclose the connection on the posts from his personal account. The FTC contends that one cannot assume that consumers would have seen his posts on the official account and would have been aware of the fact that he was a paid endorser (Federal Trade Commission 2015).

Another common scenario is when a company gives out free samples of a product to consumers, one of whom decides to write a favorable review or comment on social media. Once again a material connection does not exist because the company gave these samples free of charge to many consumers, without any expectation of a favorable endorsement. The focus of the FTC's Guides is when the company pays or gives something of value to a consumer *in return for* a favorable mention on social media (Federal Trade Commission 2013a).

Who Is Responsible?

The FTC Guidelines themselves do not have the force of law. However, any practice that is deemed to be inconsistent with or in violation of the guides may result in law enforcement actions. The FTC can and does conduct investigations and has the power to bring cases involving such endorsements under Section 5 of the FTC Act (Unfair or Deceptive Acts or Practices) (Federal Trade Commission 2015). This raises the question, "In the instance of a violation of the FTC Act, who exactly is responsible, the company or the endorser?" If law enforcement is required, the primary focus will be on advertisers, their ad agencies, and public relations company involved. However, the account holder or endorser could also be held accountable (Federal Trade Commission 2013a). For that reason, both brand marketers and endorsers need to be aware of these guidelines. Brand marketers should monitor all posts made by endorsers to ensure that each contains a clear and conspicuous disclosure. Until recently, the cases investigated by the FTC have not resulted in fines. Instead, a series of conditions were imposed on each company. Common conditions include the development of an internal compliance system, submission of regular reports to the FTC to demonstrate compliance—a process to educate social influencers on the guidelines—and a requirement to cut off payments to those social endorsers who fail to comply. These conditions can be and have been imposed on some companies for as much as 20 years (Coffee 2016; Roberts 2016). However, in the case of Teami, in 2018, the FTC had warned the company about the placement of their disclosures. Failure to address this led the FTC to impose a $15.2 million judgment against the company in 2020. The judgment was partially suspended due to the company's financial condition. In place, a $1 million fine was imposed and warning letters were sent to all of the endorsers (Williams 2020). It appears that the "honeymoon period" when companies were given a warning for their indiscretions is over.

The FTC's Endorsement Guidelines for Clear and Conspicuous Disclosures

The FTC's 2009 Guide to Endorsements and Testimonials focuses primarily on *when* to make disclosures (material connections). In 2013, the FTC released the *.Com Disclosures* report with updated guidance that now included *how* to make effective disclosures (WOMMA 2014). Both documents help businesses and endorsers avoid deceptive acts and advocate for clear and conspicuous disclosures. Whereas there is no set formula for creating a clear and conspicuous disclosure, the *.Com Disclosures* report does provide some guiding principles for marketers to ensure that

LEGAL AND REGULATORY ISSUES 163

 Guidelines for clear and conspicuous disclosures

Placement and proximity
- Place disclosure close to the claim
- Avoid pop-up disclosures
- Restrict hyperlinked disclosures to space constrained platforms

Prominence
- Make disclosure prominent
- Font size at least as large as the message
- Where possible use contrasting colors for the disclosure and message
- Do not bury the disclosure in text

Distracting factors
- Avoid all distracting factors, such as graphics, sound, and additional text

Repetition
- Repeat disclosure if there are multiple entry points to the blog or video endorsements
- Consumers must be exposed to the entire disclosure
- Repeated endorsements require repeated disclosures

Multimedia
- Match audio endorsements with audio disclosures
- Video and text disclaimers to be displayed for a sufficient duration for consumers to notice, read, and understand them

Language
- Language should be understandable-simple, straightforward, clear language, and syntax
- Avoid legalese
- Avoid technical jargon

Figure 7.1 Guidelines for clear and conspicuous disclosures

disclosures are communicated effectively (see Figure 7.1). In evaluating whether a particular disclosure is clear and conspicuous, the FTC offers the following considerations:

Placement and proximity: A disclosure is deemed to be more effective if it is placed as close as possible to the claim it qualifies. For example, if the endorsement is in the form of a tweet or status update on Facebook, the disclosure can be placed at the beginning or the end of the message. Pop-ups, which are blocked on many, but not all (e.g., blogs) social platforms, should be avoided. If the endorsement appears on a blog or personal website, it should be placed on the same page and as close as possible to the claim. If the disclosure is lengthy or the consumer has to scroll down to read it, then the consumer should be alerted via text or through visual cues (e.g., "see below for important information about this post/message"). Hyperlinks disclosures should be avoided for two reasons. First, a hyperlink is likely to take a consumer away from the claim, and therefore, disregards the requirement for proximity. Second, the consumer is often not informed on why it is important for him or her to click on the link. Hyperlinking a single word (e.g., "disclaimer" or "details") or phrase (e.g., "terms and conditions" or "more information") within the text may not be effective. These approaches may not alert the consumer to the nature of the information and its significance. As a result, motivation to and the likelihood of clicking on the link and being exposed to the disclosure are reduced. However, on space-constrained platforms, where it is necessary but impossible to include a lengthy disclosure, a hyperlinked disclosure may be used. The hyperlinked disclosure needs to be clearly labeled, using an easy-to-understand language and be sufficiently prominent, so that that it is obvious, unavoidable, and conveys the importance of the information to which it leads (e.g., "Brand Relationship Statement") (Federal Trade Commission 2013b). Asterisks (*) or other symbols by themselves may not be effective. In summary, hyperlinked disclosures should only be used as an absolute last resort. If the disclosure can be placed in close proximity to the claim, it should be.

Prominence: Each disclosure should be prominently displayed. That is, it should be noticeable to the consumer. The disclosure should be in a font size at least as large as the message. If the platform permits it, the disclosure can be presented in a contrasting color to make the disclosure more noticeable. The disclosure should not be buried in any lengthy text where it may go unnoticed. In the Teami example, endorsers posted a picture of themselves on Instagram holding the product and boasted about the wonderful results the tea had on their well-being. In many cases, these endorsers did include a disclosure (e.g., #teamipartner). However, given the length of the text on their post and the characteristics of the Instagram platform, consumers would have needed to click on the "more" button to read the entire narrative and disclosure. The placement, proximity, and prominence of the disclosure did not meet the FTC guidelines. This could have been easily avoided by placing the disclosure earlier in the posting.

Distracting factors: If the message contains distracting factors such as graphics, sound, text, and so on, the consumer may not notice the disclosure. Therefore, extreme care should be used when adding these features to the message. Avoid all distracting factors.

Repetition: Repetition makes it more likely that a consumer will notice and understand a disclosure. Repetition is particularly important if there are multiple entry points to a website, blog, or video. Consumers must be exposed to the entire disclosure, not just a portion of it. It is insufficient to endorse a product multiple times but only be exposed to a disclosure once. If a consumer is going to be exposed to repeated claims or endorsements, then the disclosure too should be repeated.

Multimedia: In the case where the endorser uses audio claims (e.g., in a video or podcast), then the disclosure should also be offered in an audio format. Video and text disclaimers should be displayed for a sufficient duration for consumers to notice, read, and understand them.

Language: The disclaimer should be simple, straightforward, and presented in a clear language and syntax. Endorsers need to avoid the use of legalese or technical jargon.

Commonly Used Method of Disclosure

The requirement for understandable language seems relatively simple and straightforward—you need to communicate your material connection in layman's terms. This may be as simple as stating verbally or in text *"I received XXXXX for this post," "This post was paid for by XYZ,"* or *"Paid for by XYZ."* This language may be appropriate for platforms that do not have message length constraints (e.g., blogs, YouTube), but they are problematic on sites that limit the length or duration of each message. Therefore, marketers need to be creative in crafting succinct endorsed messages (e.g., #PaidAd = 7 characters or #PaidPost = 9 characters).

The FTC offers some strategies to overcome this problem. The FTC suggests that in space-constrained messages, disclosing a material connect may be achieved by using abbreviations such as "Ad" for advertisement and "Paid" for a paid message or post. This is a common strategy on Twitter. See Figure 7.2 for an example of a tweet created to promote the Snickers candy bar. Notice that the inclusion of the "ad" but also consider the placement of the disclosure. Is there a possibility that this could go unnoticed?

Snickers. You're not you when you are hungry. At least I know I'm not. #snickers. ad. snickers.com/Product/Snicke...

2:12 PM - 28 May 2016

Figure 7.2 Twitter disclosure 1

The FTC acknowledges that short-form disclosures may not be adequate for all readers, as some may not understand the meaning of these abbreviations (Federal Trade Commission 2013b). An academic study of 167 Twitter users confirmed that consumers do, in fact, have difficulty understanding the intended meaning of popular disclosures. In this study, researchers examined three commonly used short-form disclosures: Ad (short for advertisement), Spon (short for sponsorship), and Samp (short for sample), and two long-form disclosures—Paid and Endorser. The findings of the study revealed that of the three short-form disclosures, "Ad" was the easiest for consumers to understand. For the long-form disclosures, "Endorser" was the most effective in communicating a material connection between the individual posting the tweet and the brand mentioned in the message. The researchers concluded that full words (e.g., "sponsored") are preferable to abbreviations (e.g., "Spon"). In the case of long-form disclosures, such as "Paid," the researchers recommend changing this to "Paid Ad" (Burkhalter, Wood, and Tryce 2014). "Contest" and "Sweepstakes" are other commonly used disclosures when an endorser posts a message in return for entry into a draw.

In addition to using abbreviations, another common strategy is the inclusion of hashtags to attempt to draw the consumers' attention to the fact that the word (e.g., Ad) is not part of the actual message. For example, it is not uncommon to see #Ad or #Sponsored included in a social post. See Figure 7.3 for an example. In this instance, the endorser has used #ad. But once again, do you think that this may go unnoticed?

Whereas this may be effective in some social media platforms, there are other platforms where hashtags are used in abundance, making it easy for the disclosure to get lost in the post. In such instances, the disclosure may not meet the FTC's guideline of being prominent. A good example of this

LEGAL AND REGULATORY ISSUES 167

Summertime sippin' with some delicious @sparklingice. Show me how you #FlavorUp #ad bit.ly/1VkhEfC

Figure 7.3 Twitter disclosure 2

I have fallen in love with this new energy drink!!!! Can't believe how good it tastes.💜💜💜 #thebest #givememore fav flavor is cherry lots of #energy #mojo #toogoodtobetrue gotta try #ad #cool #hot #nextbestthing #somuchenergy #bam #ilovecherry #musthave #wherehaveyoubeenallmylife #canihavesome #tasty

Figure 7.4 Instagram disclosure

(PAID AD)Sharing my newest @Walgreens Hawaiian Tropic favs just in time for Memorial Day! #alohatherapy

Figure 7.5 Twitter disclosure in caps with parentheses

is Instagram, where due to the liberal 2,200 character limit, hashtags are used extensively. How quickly can you spot the disclosure in Figure 7.4?

Even in the Twitter example offered in Figures 7.2 and 7.3, it could be argued that the disclosure is not prominent and may be overlooked. For platforms where there is a strong likelihood that consumers will miss the disclosure, and may not be able to understand, it may be appropriate to create a disclosure using full words, place the disclosure at the beginning of the message, and to use an additional strategy to draw attention to it (e.g., all capital letters or asterisks). See Figures 7.5 and 7.6 for examples. In Figure 7.5, the endorser has posted the disclosure in all caps surrounded in parenthesis. The disclosure is longer, making it easier to understand. Its placement at the beginning of the message helps to draw attention to it.

Figure 7.6 Facebook disclosure in caps with asterisks

Figure 7.7 Disclosure as part of the message

In Figure 7.6, we see a similar approach, except for this time, instead of parentheses, attention is drawn to by the addition of asterisks.

Another strategy is to rewrite the message so that the disclosure is included as part of the endorsement copy (Figure 7.7).

Industry Regulations

In addition to the FTC Guidelines for Clear and Conspicuous Disclosures, businesses need to follow guidelines that apply to their industry and profession. There are many highly regulated industries and professions for which there are specific guidelines regarding the use of social media in general and the online endorsements specifically. These include, but are not limited to, the banking and finance, medical, pharmaceutical, and health care industries (Lagu et al. 2008). In 2019 Evolus, the manufacturer of Jeuveau, a rival to Botox, hosted an event in Cancun, Mexico. The company flew top plastic surgeons and cosmetic dermatologists to the Ritz-Carlton to attend an "advisory board meeting." The doctors were treated to lavish dinners, poolside drinks, and gifts. More than a dozen doctors posted positive reviews of the product on their social media using the company preferred hashtag #newtox. Some of these doctors had over 180,000 followers (Thomas 2019). None of them disclosed that Evolus had paid for the trip. Evolus contended that these posts were not in violation of the FTC rules as "doctors were compensated only for their medical advice." The FTC disagreed. These doctors were treated to a free trip and gifts and thereby a material connection exists. The absence of disclosures aside, the all-expenses-paid weekend "carried echoes of an earlier, anything-goes era of pharmaceutical marketing that the industry largely abandoned after a series of scandals and billion-dollar fines." In addition to the policing of the promotion of medical products by the FTC, the FDA (Federal Drug Administration) also requires that all endorsements of products must include at least one approved use of the drug, the generic name of the drug, and all risks associated with using the drug (The Fashion Law 2019).

Employees on Social Media

So far, we have offered examples of celebrities, everyday consumers, and social influencers to endorse brands on social media. You may be wondering, what about employees? If a business encourages employees to talk about the company or individual brands on social media, or has implemented an employee advocacy program, do they need to include a disclosure? The answer to this depends if they are using the official brand account or their personal account. If employees are discussing the company on the company's official account, they do not need to disclose. However, if they are discussing the company on their personal account, they do need to disclose their connection. There is a material connection between the employee and the company, and not all of the people who see the post from the personal account may be aware of that connection. Even if an employee is answering a question on social media, he or she must disclose his or her connection with the brand (Federal Trade Commission 2013a).

> Advertising agency Deutsch LA created a marketing campaign on behalf of their client, Sony. The campaign was to promote Sony's new handheld gaming device, the PlayStation Vita. One campaign strategy was to encourage users to tweet positive statements about the Sony device using the hashtag #GameChanger (Beck 2014). In this case, consumers were not offered any consideration for sharing

(Continues)

> their positive feedback via Twitter. Thus, a material connection did not exist between the brand and their consumers. However, not all of the positive tweets originated from consumers; some originated from employees of Deutsch LA (the advertising agency behind the campaign). See the problem? A material connection did exist—an employment relationship between the employee and Deutsch, who in turn had a contractual relationship with Sony. The Deutsch LA employees failed to disclose their material connection. After the FTC had conducted an investigation, Deutsch settled. Needless to say, the agency no longer represents Sony (Beck 2015b). There is an important lesson here—do not assume that your advertising agency is aware of and adhering to the FTC Endorsement Guidelines.

Another commonly asked question is, "What if my employee has his or her place of occupation listed in the bio of his or her Twitter or the About section of Facebook. Is it still necessary to disclose?" To answer this, simply ask yourself, "Do I know the names of the employers for all of my Facebook friends and Twitter followers?" (Answer: You don't). Therefore, disclosing a material connection in the biographical section of any social media account is an insufficient method of disclosure. Think about what it would take to read an employment disclosure found in a bio. A consumer would have to click on the endorser's name, which, through a hyperlink, will take him or her to the endorser's home page where the bio or about sections are located. Most consumers will not take this extra step. As such, the employee endorser should disclose his or her material connection in each post (Federal Trade Commission 2013a). An alternative strategy is to have the employee create a separate account for work purposes with the name of the brand incorporated in the account name or handle, for example, "@DaveFromDell." In the case of LinkedIn, the name of the employer appears alongside the endorser's name. However, this does not guarantee that the consumer will read this information, as it may not meet the guidelines for prominence, placement, and proximity. Also, many employees list the parent company name on LinkedIn. The reader may not be familiar with the parent company, and therefore, may not realize that a relationship exists between the endorser and the brand

(Federal Trade Commission 2013a). For example, not many people know Sun Capital Partners Inc. is the owner of Boston Markets (restaurant), Hannah Anderson (apparel), and Flamingo Horticulture (consumer goods). The method of the disclosure can vary depending on the social media platform on which it appears (e.g., "Disclosure: I work for XYZ," XYZ employee), but it needs to meet the requirements for clear and conspicuous disclosures (Castillo 2014).

Platform-Specific Templates

Some social media platforms have created a selection of branded content tools to help businesses build connections, develop partnerships with influencers, and support the FTC's efforts to ensure adequate disclosure of material connections. For example, Instagram encourages content creators (e.g., influencers) to convert their account to a creator or business account, providing them with access to various tools to help them promote brands. One of these tools helps communicate that a paid partnership exists between the individual and the brand mentioned in their post. When the creator creates a post and tags the brand, the words "Paid Partnership with (brand name)" will appear at the top of the post. See Figure 7.8 for an example. Instagram's sister platform Facebook offers a similar feature. At the time of publication, other popular social media platforms such as Twitter and Snapchat did not provide this feature. Instagram and Facebook's inclusion of this branded content tool is undoubtedly a step in the right direction in facilitating transparency. However, it is not a perfect solution. These tools do not currently meet all of the FTC guidelines for

Figure 7.8 Instagram Paid Sponsored Post from account @codyrigsby

clear and conspicuous disclosures. Even though the "Paid Partnership" disclosure is prominent and in easy-to-understand language, it may not pass the placement and proximity test. The disclosure appears at the top of the post rather than close to the claim/endorsement. Readers tend to ignore the top of posts. For this reason, we recommend that content creators include a disclosure close to the content in addition to using this tool (Davies 2020). See the text included in Figure 7.8 ("I teamed up with my friends @chobani …").

Commonly Asked Questions

Admittedly, understanding and adhering to the FTC Guidelines is easier said than done. Also, social media continually presents new problems and situations that test our understanding of these important rules. To help ease you into FTC compliance, following are the answers to some additional commonly asked questions.

Material Connection and Compensation

Q: "Is there a monetary threshold for disclosing a relationship? What if we (the business, for example, a coffee shop) are only offering a 'token of appreciation' for an online recommendation or endorsement, such as a free cup of coffee or a dollar-off coupon?"

A: When it comes to material connections, there is no monetary threshold. The key is whether the likelihood that the "token of appreciation" will affect the weight and credibility of the endorsement. One might argue that a cup of coffee is not such a sufficient weight to influence a consumer, but a month's supply of free coffee may be viewed differently (Beck 2015c). It is both easier and in everyone's best interest to adopt a consistent practice and habit of disclosing on each platform, regardless of the actual or perceived value of the incentive.

Q: "For a material connection to exist, does there have to a monetary value attached to the incentive? For example, what if I move a customer to the top of a waiting list, invite him or her to a product launch event, seat him or her at a better table in my restaurant?"

A: There does not need to be a financial arrangement for a material connection to exist. In this case, the incentive is a special access privilege. The FTC states that if the customer is offered privileges in return for social media mentions, then yes, there is a material connection, and it should be disclosed (Federal Trade Commission 2013a). Remember, an incentive with no financial value may still affect the credibility of an endorsement (Federal Trade Commission 2013).

Q: "If I offer my customers a discount on a future purchase, or offer to enter them into a draw to win a prize, do they need to disclose?"

A: The customer is still being incentivized to post, and therefore, a material connection exists, and a disclosure should be included. Similar to "tokens of appreciation," the value of this incentive will determine the importance of the disclosure. The greater the incentive, the greater the importance of the disclosure, and the more likely a business and endorser will come under scrutiny for failing to disclose. For instance, a significant discount or entry into a draw to win a substantial item is more likely to be questioned than one where the discount or prize is very small (Federal Trade Commission 2013a). The challenge here lies at the interpretation of "significant" and "substantial."

Endorsers/Advocates/Influencers

Q: "I have a well-known spokesperson (noncelebrity) who endorses my product in print ads. Does he or she now need to start disclosing when he or she endorses us through his or her Twitter and Facebook accounts?"

A: The answer to this depends on whether his or her social media followers are aware that he or she already endorses your product. If there is a chance that his or her followers are unaware, then yes, he or she would need to disclose his or her connection in each of his or her posts (Beck 2015c).

Q: "What if the person who endorses my product is a well-known celebrity and has appeared in some traditional advertisements (TV, print, and so on)? If he or she starts mentioning us on social media, does he or she need to disclose?"

A: If the celebrity is a known endorser of your product, then it may not be necessary to disclose the connection when posting on social media. However, if a significant number of the people who follow his or her social media accounts do not know that he or she is an endorser, then he or she will need to disclose (Federal Trade Commission 2013a). Take, for example, a celebrity who is a spokesperson for a regional business appearing only in regional TV and print advertisements. Knowledge of his or her affiliation with the business may be geographically confined to areas where these advertisements air. His or her social media followers may be more geographically disbursed.

Remember, just because some consumers may be aware of the connection between the endorser and the brand does not mean that all consumers are (Federal Trade Commission 2015). An act is considered deceptive if it leads to "a significant minority" (Federal Trade Commission 2015).

Q: I am an influencer, and I often post about products that I paid for and those that I received as a free sample. Do I need to state that how I got the product in my posting?

A: If you are paid for it or the company gave out free samples to a number of its customers, you do not need to state that. The FTC is only concerned about sponsored endorsements—where an arrangement/understanding exists between you and the company that you will mention the product in return for giving you something of value (Federal Trade Commission 2013).

Q: What if I return the product after I have finished using it? Is a disclosure still required?

A: That may depend on the product and how long you had to use it. Take, for instance, having access to a new car for a weekend or an inexpensive home appliance for a month. In both cases, your posting might affect the credibility your readers give to your recommendation. It is safer to disclose (Federal Trade Commission 2017).

Q: I often get products sent to me as "gifts" from various companies. I am under no obligation to post about them on my social media. But if I do post, is a disclosure required?

A: If a reader is likely to think differently about your post knowing that you were given the item for free, you should disclose. Given that it is unlikely that you will know your reviews impact on all those who see it, it would be wise to include a disclosure (Federal Trade Commission 2017).

Q: Do I have to post something about the product for it to be considered an endorsement?

A: Posting a picture or a video could convey that you approve of a product. Words/text is not necessary. Images alone can represent approval. If you have a relationship with the company, then you need to disclose it (Federal Trade Commission 2017).

Q: If I post a picture of myself on Instagram and tag the brand of clothing I am wearing, do I need to disclose?

A: Tagging a brand is considered an endorsement. Don't assume that because you have tagged the brand, your followers will interpret this to mean that you have a relationship with the brand. They may not. If you have a relationship with the brand, then you must disclose that in your posting. If there is no relationship, then a disclosure is not necessary (Federal Trade Commission 2017).

Q: What if I simply "like" a posting on Facebook or share a link on Twitter?

A: Utilizing the features available on individual platforms such as emoticons, likes, shares, retweets, and links may convey your endorsement. Utilizing these features may be perceived as deceptive if you have a relationship with the company. If you have entered into a relationship with the company then you need to include a disclosure. Advertisers shouldn't encourage endorsements using these features and influencers should avoid using them (Federal Trade Commission 2017).

Employee Endorsements

Q: Can I recommend or mention products/services that my company offers on my personal social media accounts? My family and friends know who I work for and the name of the company is listed in my bio.

A: First, you cannot assume that all of your followers know the name of your employer. You cannot assume that all of your followers have or will read the contents of your bio. Therefore, you should disclose this relationship. A simple way to do this is by incorporating the disclosure into the message. For example, "the company I work for has a great new product …"

Q: Can I "like" or "share" some of my company's posts with my social networks without including a disclosure?

A: Similar to a previous example (under influencers) utilizing the features available on individual platforms such as emoticons, likes, shares, retweets, and links may convey your endorsement. As an employee, you have a material connection with the company. Utilizing these features may be perceived as deceptive if you have not disclosed your relationship with your followers. Employers shouldn't encourage employees to use these features and employees should avoid using them (Federal Trade Commission 2017).

Q: Is "#employee" an acceptable form of disclosure?

A: Not all followers may understand what is meant by #employee or how it relates to the message. A better way of disclosing your relationship is with "#ABC_ employee" or "employee of ABC" (Federal Trade Commission 2017).

How to Disclosure

Q: "Do I need to hire a lawyer to write these disclosures?"

A: If your disclosure is written in clear, easy-to-understand language and avoids legalese and technical jargon, then you do not need a lawyer (Federal Trade Commission 2013a).

Q: "What are some of the phrases we can use to disclose a material connection?"

A: The type and length of the phrase will vary depending on the platform. Aim for disclosures that include full words rather than abbreviations. Disclosures can be presented in all capital letters, contrasting colors, or accompanied by symbols (e.g., #, ***) to draw attention to them.

Q: "I cannot fit a message and disclosure in a Tweet, what do I do?"

A: If there is not enough room, then you should rewrite your message, so that you can include a disclosure. Character or space limitations are not a valid excuse for excluding a disclosure (Beck 2015c). Furthermore, disclosures must be present on all messages, regardless of the device (e.g., computer, tablet, cell phone) used by the intended audience (WOMMA 2014).

Q: What if my message is long and truncated so that you have to click on "more" to read the entire message and see the disclosure?

A: Truncating a long message is a common practice in many platforms including Instagram. If this is the case, the disclosure should appear at the beginning of the message. Followers should not have to click on "more" to locate the disclosure (Federal Trade Commission 2017).

Q: Can I include a hyperlink or button that says something like "Disclosure" or "Legal" which will take the follower to a different location where the disclosure is explained in full?

A: No. Hyperlinks do not meet the FTC guideline proximity. It also does not convey the importance of the information. There is no guarantee that the follower will click on the link and read the disclosure (Federal Trade Commission 2017).

Q: "What if the social media posts are posted in another language. What language should the disclosure be in?"

A: The disclosure is to be presented in the same language as the endorsement (Federal Trade Commission 2013a).

Q: "What is the best way to disclose in a video?"

A: It is advisable to have the disclosure at the beginning of the video. The disclosure can be communicated verbally and appear on the screen in text. It is important that the text disclosure is visible long enough for the viewer to read it in its entirety. When posting videos to platforms such as YouTube, care should be taken to ensure that the disclosure is not obstructed by advertisements. For long videos or even live streams, where viewers can enter and exit a video at any time, it is necessary to include multiple disclosures throughout the video or stream (Federal Trade Commission 2013a). Avoid including the disclosure in the video description as it can be easily missed.

Q: "Do all types of social media posts promoting a brand need include a disclosure? What if the post is a photo or a video without any text, do these need a disclosure?"

A: Positive sentiment and endorsement for a product can be communicated in many ways, including through a simple photograph. Take, for example, the case of Jason Peterson. Peterson, an advertising executive, was reportedly given a first-class ticket to Iceland and $15,000 in cash in return for sharing four images of Dom Perignon with his 300,000+ Instagram followers. In another example, freelance photographer Alina Tsvor shared a photograph of her flight with Chicago Helicopter Experience with her 55,000+ Instagram followers in return for free helicopter rides for her and her friends. In both of these cases, the advocates relied on images to communicate their endorsement. Disclosures should have been included (Mann 2014).

Q: How do I disclose on Snapchat, Instagram Stories, or TikTok?

A: Superimpose the disclosure over the image/video. To ensure the disclosure meets FTC requirements, consider how long the disclosure appears on the screen—how long will it take to read? How much competing text is there—is your disclosure free of distracting factors? How large is the text font and how well does it contrast against the image—is it prominent? Avoid using audio-only disclosures as people often use these platforms without sound (Federal Trade Commission 2017).

Q: Can we incorporate the company name into the disclosure (e.g., #StarbucksAd)?

A: Don't assume that people will understand the significance of the "ad" particularly when combined with another word. "Starbucks Ad" would be better; "Starbucks Advertisement" is even better. Furthermore, the disclosure component of the hashtag (Ad) may go unnoticed particularly if there is more than one hashtag in the posting. Disclosures must be easy to notice (prominent, free of distracting factors).

Q: "Do product reviews that appear on my company website or websites such as Yelp need to include disclosures?"

A: That depends on whether or not there is a material connection between the consumer posting the review and the brand he or she is referencing. If the reviewer received a benefit or incentive for writing the review, then yes, a disclosure is necessary. If no benefit or incentive was offered then, no material connection exists and the reviewer does not need to disclose (Federal Trade Commission 2013a).

Q: "When an endorser posts on the brand's official account, does he or she need to disclose?"

A: If the post only appears on the official brand account, then the answer is no. However, if he or she is also posting from his or her personal account, then yes, he or she needs to disclose. Alternatively, he or she can create a separate social media account for these posts where the brand name is incorporated in the account name or handle. For example "@JoeFromPepsi."

The importance of complying with the FTC and industry guidelines for sWOM cannot be understated. Your company needs to ensure that all employees and endorsers understand the importance of and appropriate method of disclosure. This information is often documented in your company's social media policy.

Social Media Policy

The first step to mitigating risk is to develop and implement a social media policy. The next part of this chapter will offer a framework for developing a policy. In the interest of full disclosure, we are not lawyers, and therefore, we recommend that when preparing your policy, you consult your legal department. The framework presented here is offered as a general guide and may need to be modified to fit your company.

What Is a Social Media Policy and Why Do We Need One?

A social media policy is a code of conduct developed and approved by senior management. The purpose of a social media policy is to communicate how the company views social media, and how they will use it in a business context. Guidelines contained within the policy provide direction on how to use social media. These guidelines are often created based on a set of best practices. They protect the company, company employees, and their clients from public relations and legal crises and help the company present and maintain a positive and consistent brand identity. A well-written set of guidelines should also empower employees, providing them with the confidence they need to utilize social media effectively. For the most part, a social media policy is about educating employees to simply use common sense when using social media.

A typical policy will, at a minimum, include information on the social platforms the company has approved for business use, who is authorized to speak on behalf of the company, what content may or may not be posted, how to share content, and general rules of engagement. The following section offers some guidelines on developing a policy.

Developing a Social Media Policy and Guidelines

Step 1: What Is Your Purpose?

The first step is to determine your purpose for using social media. Is social media to be used purely as a marketing communications tool—a tool to inform, persuade, and build relationships with existing and potential consumers—or does it serve a larger purpose? Do you want it to be integrated into multiple functional areas (e.g., HR, purchasing, sales)? Are you striving to be a social business (see Chapter 3)? Clearly articulating your purpose for using social media is like planning a road trip. First, you decide where it is you want to go—why are you using social media? Then, you plan the best way of getting there and what resources and tools you will need (e.g., what platforms you will need, who will use them, what they need to know)? Without a clear purpose, you are likely to develop an ineffective policy. Common reasons for using social media in a business setting include but are not limited to:

1. Increasing brand awareness
2. Strengthening the brand's reputation
3. Sharing and amplifying stories of success with external audiences
4. Building and strengthening relationships with existing and prospective consumers
5. Listening to and learning from consumers (i.e., marketing research)
6. Engaging with vendors
7. Improving customer service
8. Increasing conversions (i.e., sales, lead generation)
9. Recruiting and retaining high-quality employees
10. Fostering pride among employees

It is likely that your company will have more than one purpose. Articulating your purpose and putting it down on paper will help you to identify appropriate social media platforms and content for your policy.

Step 2: Examine Your Company Culture

The next step, examining your company culture, begins by revisiting your company mission and values. Let these guide your policy-development process. Take, for instance, the Coca-Cola Company's mission: "To refresh the world; To inspire moments of optimism and happiness; To create value and make a difference." The Coca-Cola Company's values include leadership, collaboration, integrity, accountability, passion, diversity, and quality (The Coca-Cola Company 2016a). Their social media policy, which is available in company's website, embraces the corporate mission and values, encouraging employees to "Have fun, but be smart." To "use sound judgment and common sense," to "adhere to the Company's values" (The Coca-Cola Company 2016b).

Next, consider who will be using social media and the beliefs about social media that exist within your company. Do you have executive buy-in? How do your employees feel about social media? What social media platforms do they use? Are you creating an employee advocacy program? Do you plan to use social influencers? The answers to these questions will help you to determine how detailed your policy will need to be, the amount of education and training required, and who you should invite to be a member of your social media advisory board.

Step 3: Create a Social Media Advisory Board—A Center of Excellence

A Social Media Advisory Board, or if you are looking for a name with little more pizzazz, a Social Media Center of Excellence, is a group of individuals whose purpose is to craft the social media policy and appropriate guidelines. Charlene Li, CEO and Principal Analyst at Altimeter Group, a research and strategic consulting company, contends that the Center of Excellence is a company's moral compass. The center collectively decides which platforms the company will use, creates policies on how to use these platforms, identifies best practices, and provides training for employees and any third party who may be posting on behalf of the company (e.g., social influencers), and ensures that the brand voice is appropriate and consistent (Hootsuite University 2013). The center should also sample social media posts within and across each of the company's social media accounts to ensure that the content, language, and tone is consistent with the company's brand personality and brand voice.

The size and composition of your company's center should be based on your purpose for using social media (Step 1). For instance, if you are only using social media for marketing purposes, the large majority of your center will comprise marketing employees. If you are a social business, then your center should include representatives from all areas of your business (i.e., HR, Finance, Marketing, and so on). Even if your purpose is restricted to a particular business function, such as marketing, it is wise to have additional representation. An outsider may offer a different perspective, play "devil's advocate," and reduce the occurrence of group-think. A center may also include experts (industry and social media) as well as consumers. You may decide to include a member of your legal team to navigate potential legal landmines. However, it is important to remember that legal team is a participant in the process, not the sole driver. If you choose not to add a member of your legal team to your center, you will still need them to review your policy prior to implementation. Above all, when forming your center, it is important to recruit "social-media- friendly" people. Seek out the "social media evangelists," those individuals who see the value in social media and who will become internal advocates for the policy.

During the early stages of policy development, the center may need to meet on a regular basis. Once the policy has been developed and employees trained, meetings may be less frequent. The work undertaken by the center will also evolve over time. When the policy is first introduced, the center may work as a centralized body, vetting planned social media activities and monitoring online activities. As the workforce becomes more skilled, the approval and monitoring process may become decentralized. The center may only need to meet a few times a year to review and update policies. We recommend meeting at least twice a year.

Step 4: Research

Once the Center of Excellence has been formed, the next step is to conduct research. The research phase involves reviewing existing business policies, researching best practices, identifying potential laws and regulations, and benchmarking against other companies. It is advisable to create a centralized system for posting and sharing information collected. An internal website, Google Documents, or Dropbox folder are all suitable options.

Review Existing Policies

The first step is to determine if there are existing policies in place that address the use of social media in the workplace for business or personal purposes (e.g., HR policies). If policies exist, the center needs to decide whether the existing policies can be amended or whether new policies are required. As social media is integrated into multiple functional areas; it is likely that existing policies will need to be updated. For example, if a business decides to use social media as a recruiting tool, current human resources policies are likely to be impacted and will need to be updated. The new social media policy crafted by the center may reference the use of social media for recruiting; however, the recruiting policies that reside in HR may be silent on social media or offer conflicting guidelines. For this reason, it is advisable to review all the existing policies to determine those that need to be updated so as to avoid conflicting policies.

Best Practices

Social media platforms are constantly in a state of flux. Platforms such as Facebook frequently update their interface and news-feed algorithms to enhance user experience (and maximize revenue). The manner and purpose behind consumers' use of social media also change over time.

Best practices can be categorized into two areas: rules of engagement and platform approach. Rules of engagement are appropriate behaviors for social posting and engaging with consumers on social media. The mission and values of the business will guide the creation of these approved behaviors, as will the rules of professional communication etiquette. To illustrate, some of Best Buy's values are respect, humility, and integrity (Best Buy 2020). Best Buy's social media policy and guidelines call on employees to be smart, respectful, and human. Employees are required to disclose their affiliation with Best Buy, act responsibility and ethically, and to honor differences (Best Buy Social Media Policy 2020). Rules of engagement can also be formulated from a variety of external sources including industry and consumer expectations, published research, social media experts, professional and industry organizations (e.g., WOMMA.org), and societal expectations.

Platform approach refers to appropriate methods of communicating and engagement on specific social media platforms. Approaches to using specific platforms can be general (what type of content can be posted on which platform) or specific (the best days of the week and times of the day to post). Similar to rules of engagement, these approaches are formulated from a variety of sources, including an analysis of those activities that generate the greatest level of engagement of the company's account (views, positive comments, likes, shares, downloads, and so on) and published research reports (academic, industry, and organizational). Please note that companies often publish an abridged version of their social policy and guidelines on the company website. It is unlikely that this public version of the policy will include how the company will approach each platform. A more detailed document containing guidelines for how employees should use specific platforms may exist offline.

Laws and Regulations

Federal and state laws, as well as industry regulations, may apply to social media. The majority of these fall into three categories: intellectual property, employment-related issues, and marketing activities. A policy will, at a minimum, provide a statement requiring that employees comply with government laws and industry regulations. A list of these laws and regulations is often included. A more robust policy will include details of or links to a detailed description of each law and regulation, with instructions and guidelines to ensure compliance. The closer a company moves toward being a social business, the greater the number of laws and regulations to which the company, their employees, and third parties must comply. Remember to address the FTC guidelines for disclosure of material connections. The Social Media Center of Excellence should seek legal advice on laws and regulations that apply to their industry and social media activities.

Your company is also bound to the terms of service for each social media platform (Facebook, Twitter, and so on) that you use. As such, platform-specific terms of service and policies should be reviewed in advance to identify any potential obstacles (Smith and Russell 2016).

Benchmarking

The task of developing a social media policy and guidelines can, at first, appear overwhelming. But there is no need to reinvent the wheel. There are many examples of comprehensive, well-written social media policies available online. Begin by contacting industry associations for sample policies and guidelines. Next, research competitors to identify the breadth and depth of their social policies and guidelines. Finally, it may be helpful to review the policies of leading corporations, such as IBM, Microsoft, The Coca-Cola Company, Intel, and Adidas, which are available on each company's website. Keep in mind, the policies and guidelines available online may be an abridged version.

Step 5: Draft a Document and Distribute for Feedback

Drafting a policy is like writing a book. It takes time and multiple drafts to get it right. The first draft may be quite lengthy. Do not worry, remember, it is easier to reduce the size of a document than it is to add to it later. Keep the document simple. Use simple, easy-to-understand language. To reduce the need for frequent updates, try to avoid including information that may outdate quickly. Keep lengthy paragraphs to a minimum and use bullet points to emphasize key points. A draft of the policy should be submitted to your company's attorney and senior management for feedback and final approval. If the final document is large, consider developing an abridged version for easy daily reference.

The Social Media Policy: What to Include

The following is a brief overview of each section in a typical social media policy.

Policy Statement

Begin by stating the policy. In your policy statement, you should include whom the policy applies to (scope) and the reason for the policy (purpose). If appropriate, you can link the policy to the company's mission and values.

Approved Platforms

This section will list the social media platforms that the company has approved for official business purposes. These terms of services and policies of each platform should be vetted by the legal department before adoption.

Account Status

There are two categories of accounts, official accounts and unofficial accounts. Official accounts are those accounts approved, created, and managed by the company. A list of and links to all official accounts should be included in the policy document.

Unofficial accounts are created by employees, individual departments, and consumers. These accounts may include your company name or logo but were not vetted by the company, and the content that is being posted to these accounts is not being monitored. To the average consumer, these unofficial accounts may look like authorized accounts. For that reason, your company needs to decide the manner in which they handle these accounts. The policy document should clearly state how the company will address unofficial accounts.

There are three options for managing unofficial accounts.

1. Independence: Allow the account to exist and independently operate. You should carefully consider this option. By allowing these accounts to operate independently, your company has little to no control over the content. This could have negative implications for your company.
2. Compliance: Contact the account holder and encourage him or her to apply for official account status. In this case, the company will allow the account to remain as long as the account administrator abides by the company's social media guidelines. In return, the company may offer to list the page on the company website and will grant the account administrator permission to use company images and logos. Transitioning an unofficial account to become an official account may be a viable option if the account has a large following and has achieved positive results. Someone within the company will need to be responsible for monitoring the account to ensure continued compliance with company guidelines. If the account holder declines your offer to make their account official or does not respond to your request, you may decide to move to option three—termination.
3. Termination: Contact the account administrator and request that he or she remove all company intellectual property (logos, trademarks, and so on). Also, request that they must clearly indicate on the account (in the bio or account description) that this is an unofficial account and that all posts are made by a specific individual (and include his name). If the account holder fails to comply, you may want to issue a cease and desist letter. You should also file an unauthorized trademark use report with the specific platform.

Legal Issues

The policy document should, at a minimum, include a statement requiring that employees comply with federal and state laws and industry regulations. A list of these laws and regulations should be included. An additional step is to include details of or links to detailed descriptions of each law and regulation along with instructions and guidelines to ensure compliance.

Account Access

The policy document should indicate who is permitted to post on behalf of the company. If employees are required to complete training before being granted permission to post, then this should also be stated.

Account Ownership

There may be instances in which an employee creates a social media account that is granted "official account" status, yet the account was created with the employee's work e-mail address (e.g., janedoe@socialgurus.com), rather than using an administrative e-mail address (e.g., social@socialgurus.com). Common sense would dictate that once the account receives an official status that the e-mail address associated with the account would be updated. If this slips through the cracks, it may be worthwhile to include a statement that states that all accounts that have been granted official status are the property of the company. That way, if an employee leaves the company, the account ownership (login) will transfer to the company.

Brand Voice

In Chapter 3, we discussed the importance of humanizing your brand. To convey this personality, you need to develop a brand voice. Brand voice is how that personality is portrayed through communication. Creating a brand voice begins by reviewing the mission of your company to help you identify the appropriate language and tone to use in your social communications. Regarding language choice, you need to decide whether you want your posts to be written using simple or complex words, should the message be serious or fun, and should you include or avoid the use of technical jargon. Another factor related to language choice is the need to establish a consistent message tone. What is the appropriate tone that reflects your brand personality? Is it direct, personal, scientific, fun, sassy, humble, and so on? Communication is certainly not just about word choices. You must also consider the appropriate type of photographs and video. Visual components of the message must be aligned with the brand voice and accurately reflect the brand's personality. In Chapter 3, we offered the example of Taco Bell. Taco Bell's brand voice is humorous and wacky. The Taco Bell Facebook page recently contained a post titled "This just happened: I got engaged to a Doritos Locos Tacos." Accompanying the announcement was a picture of a high school student dressed in a suit proposing to a taco. On Twitter, the company posts visuals, which include funny taco gifs, and pictures of taco t-shirts, all of which support the company's brand voice. Your company may want to add a brand voice style guide as an appendix to your policy.

Best Practices: Rules of Engagement

When educating employees on how to engage with followers on social media, it helps if you include both specific directions and examples. Following are some suggested, although generic, guidelines that companies may adopt. Please note that depending on the expectations of your figure industry, your company and the laws and regulations that apply to a company may decide to elaborate on each item.

Know the Rules

Before posting content to a company account, make sure that you have read and that you understand the company's social media policy. Ensure that you are familiar with federal, state, and industry laws and regulations.

Be Yourself

Social media is a great communication and community-building tool—a place where you and your audience can share information, engage with one another, and build and maintain relationships. Write in the first person and allow your personality to show.

Be Respectful

At all times, post meaningful and respectful comments. Do not post negative comments or engage in negative conversations about competing companies. Resist the urge to respond to negative posts. Your engagement needs to be focused and professional, and should aim to add value.

Be Transparent

Be transparent about your affiliation with the company and avoid misrepresentation. If you are endorsing the company or one of their products, ensure that you include a disclosure that meets the FTC Guidelines. If you make a mistake (e.g., share inaccurate information), you need to admit it. Be upfront and quick with your correction.

Maintain Confidentiality

Do not discuss confidential or proprietary information on social media. Do not discuss or disclose business partnerships or employee information on social media.

Respect Proprietary Content

Be respectful of proprietary information and content. Do not use copyrighted materials (print, media, or any other digital files) and intellectual property without first gaining permission from the owner. Also, give credit to the source of this content in your postings.

Best Practices: Platform Approach

People are motivated to use different social media outlets for different purposes. For example, Facebook is popular for communicating with family and friends, whereas LinkedIn is more appropriate for communicating with the company and industry associates. Furthermore, each platform has its nuances that will impact how information is shared. If your company decides to restrict specific communications to particular platforms or has a preference for how that information is presented, then this should be outlined for employees. Platform approach guidelines may be appropriate when a large percentage of the workforce is permitted to post to and engage with consumers on social media. Walmart is an example of a company that offers separate guidelines for Twitter, Facebook, and Instagram (Wal-Mart Stores, Inc. 2016).

Policy Enforcement

In addition to providing rules of engagement, it is also important to explain to employees the consequences of failing to adhere to the policy or follow the guidelines. The severity of the punishment will largely depend on the infraction, ranging from a warning to termination. It is up to your company to decide on the appropriate punishment for a specific infraction. Your human resources and legal department can assist in crafting a statement for inclusion in the document.

Introducing the Policy

Once the policy has been approved by the legal department and senior management, it is ready to be presented to employees and relevant third parties. The manner in which the policy is introduced to the workforce is a function of the size and culture of the company, geographic disbursement of employees, and how social-media-savvy your employees are. The obvious place to introduce the policy and guidelines is during new employee orientation. For existing employees, an alternative strategy will be required. For a small business, a short in-person information and training session may be sufficient. For larger organizations with a more disbursed workforce, a more creative approach may be required. One suggestion is to create a short educational video (Tung 2014). Another alternative is to offer training through a series of webinars.

Whereas a four-minute video or a brief in-person information session may be sufficient for providing a general overview of the policy and guidelines, a lengthier, more detailed training session may be required for those employees authorized to post on behalf of the company (e.g., employee advocates). As an example, the computer and technology company Dell requires employees to undergo a certification process before being granted permission to post on behalf of the company. Dell created their own Social Media and Communications University (SMaC U—pronounced "smack you") to train Dell employees on the best way to use social media.

Regardless of the method of delivery—in-person, webinar, or video—the best way to develop an informed and skilled social media workforce is not just to tell them what to do, but to show them how to do it. Employees should, in a controlled environment, be given the opportunity to put it into practice what they have learned. A sound training session will use stories and examples to help employees understand the rules. It will also present them with some common scenarios to which they are asked to apply the guidelines they have learned.

To ensure FTC compliance, training should also be provided to endorsers. It is a brand's responsibility to educate and train all those who represent the brand online. As part of the endorser recruitment process, you should inform all potential endorsers that they are required to disclose their connection with the company in each and every post. You may even want to go as far as specifying the methods of disclosure that you would like them to use. To ensure compliance, you can inform endorsers that the incentive is contingent upon the disclosure being included. You also need to systematically monitor posts to ensure compliance. There should be scheduled review times and consequences for noncompliance.

When outsourcing this activity to an advertising agency, public relations company, or any third party, you should confirm that they will be following and enforcing the FTC Guidelines. Ask for regular reports to verify compliance. Outsourcing your promotional activity to an outside agency will not absolve you of your responsibility to abide by the FTC Act. Refresher training may be required periodically to keep abreast with any changes to the FTC Guides.

Periodic Review

The final step of the process is to periodically review both the policy and guidelines to ensure that they are current. It is also important to revisit the legal aspects of social media. As updates are made, refresher training for all employees will be required. Even if there have been no changes to the policy or guidelines, it is advisable to offer a brief refresher training, perhaps once a year. A short video may be an effective approach.

Copyright on Social Media

We would be remiss if we did not discuss copyright as it applies to social media, particularly ownership of photographs and videos. It is not uncommon or surprising that businesses like to reshare consumer-generated content on their page. Consumer-generated content is often viewed as more authentic and can be more persuasive than company-created content. Posting consumer content on the business's official account allows for a continuous stream of fresh content at a minimal cost. The challenge is that this content does not belong to the company. It belongs to the consumer and is therefore subject to copyright. Breaching copyright can result in legal action against the business. Here are two examples to illustrate a breach of copyright.

1. Shereen Way posted a photo on Instagram of her four-year-old daughter wearing a pair of pink Crocs sandals. Crocs took the picture from Instagram and featured it in a website gallery of user-generated photographs before asking for Ms. Way's permission. Eventually, the company did seek her permission—which she did not give. Fortunately for the Crocs company, Ms. Way did not pursue legal action (Murabayashi 2015).
2. On the 2013 anniversary of the September 11 attacks, Fox News personality Jeanie Pirro posted a status update on her Facebook page. The post was Thomas Franklin's famous photograph of New York City firefighters raising the American flag over the rubble of the World Trade Center on September 11, 2001. Included with the post was the hashtag #NeverForget. The photo owners, North Jersey Media Group, filed a lawsuit against Pirro (Zara 2015). Fox News Network LLC was later added to the suit. In 2016, Fox News and North Jersey Media Group settled ("Fox News, North Jersey Media Group End Lawsuits Through Settlement" 2016).

Image copyright implies image ownership. It is a form of legal protection automatically given to a creator when an image is snapped, saved, or drawn. It applies to photographs, digital art, maps, charts, and paintings. The copyright owner is the individual who takes a picture, records a video, or creates the art. It is not the person who owns the camera or the account owner where the item appears. When a photographer is commissioned, they often retain ownership of the item(s) but permit their client to use them according to the terms laid out in the agreement. If the business uses the content in a manner outside of the agreement, it may breach copyright.

In the case of consumer-generated posts, a company interested in using or sharing an image must seek permission from the copyright holder. If a person took the picture and posted it to their account, they are the copyright owner. But if the photo is taken by one person and posted to another person's page, then permission needs to be sought from the owner of the image, not the account owner. Just because an image is shared on a public account does not mean that image is in the public domain and therefore free to be used. Gaining permission and assigning credit to the image owner are imperative on social media. So what should a business do if they identify a photograph (or other artwork) posted on public social media and want to share that item on their business page? First, if sharing is allowed on the platform, it's typically OK to share images within the platform. Retweets, reshares, repins, or posts shared to an Instagram story automatically credit the creator. By using the share button, the owner of the account is added to the posting. For example, if you find a post from a consumer on Facebook that you would like to share with your network, check if the "Share" button is enabled. If it is, when you share it with your network, the original owner's name will be included in the post, giving them credit. If the "Share" button is not enabled or the platform you are using has no built-in feature that allows reposting, it's necessary to ask for permission. Reach out to the account owner via direct message or post in the comments section to obtain permission. But be sure to confirm that the account owner is also the owner of the image. Assuming approval is granted, credit the owner by tagging them in the post (e.g., source: @username). Another strategy is to encourage people to post their photos with a branded hashtag. For example, Airbnb asks customers to post pictures of their accommodations on social media along with the hashtag #airbnb. If the company sees a photo they would like to use, Airbnb leaves a comment in the posting asking the account owner to go to a link where they can read and agree to its terms of use. Consumers reply with #AirbnbPhoto to confirm that the company can use the image (Canning 2019).

Conclusion

When we decided to write this book, it was not our intention to provide a comprehensive guide to sWOM. If that were the case, this book would be titled "The Complete Guide to Social Word of Mouth (sWOM)." The reality is that social media is a moving target. As social media grows and evolves and social consumers change the way in which they use social so too will your strategies. The fluid nature of social media makes it challenging to write a book that will stand the test of time, at least for a few years. Instead, we wrote this book to provide you an understanding of sWOM and how you can use it within your company. We included examples of how other companies have embraced social media and sWOM to make connections, enhance their relationships with consumers, create their brand voice and build their brand identity. Although this is the end of our book, it certainly is not the end of your education on sWOM. Indeed, this is only the start of what is sure to be an interesting and hopefully rewarding direction for your company. We hope that this book has provided you with a sound foundation on sWOM and the motivation to begin this important journey. If it has, we encourage you to spread the word. #Share.

References

Abadi, M. 2019. "The Leaked Fyre Festival Investor Pitch Deck Shows How Billy McFarland Was Able to Secure Millions for the Most Overhyped Festival in History." Business Insider. www.businessinsider.com/fyre-festival-investor-pitch-deck-2019-2#it-lists-several-of-fyres-pending-corporate-partnerships-and-cites-mcfarlands-previous-company-magnises-as-a-confirmed-partner-another-partner-the-ticket-vendor-tablelist-is-suing-fy.

Allan, D. and N. Wood. 2020. *Where There's Smoke (and Mirrors) There's Fyre! Where There's Smoke (and Mirrors) There's Fyre!* https://doi.org/10.4135/9781529711226.

Beck, M. 2014. "FTC's First Twitter Disclosure Crackdown Is a Wake-Up Call." *Marketing Land.* http://marketingland.com/ftc-social-media-disclosure-110310.

Beck, M. 2015a. "Did Lord & Taylor's Instagram Influencer Campaign Cross The Line?" *Marketing Land.* Retrieved from http://marketingland.com/did-lord-taylors-instagram-influencer-campaign-cross-the-line-123961.

Beck, M. 2015b. "FTC's First Twitter Disclosure Crackdown Is a Wake-Up Call." *Marketing Land.* Retrieved from http://marketingland.com/ftc-puts-social-media-marketers-on-notice-with-updated-disclosure-guidelines-132017.

Beck, M. 2015c. "FTC Puts Social Media Marketers on Notice With Updated Disclosure Guidelines." *Marketing Land.* Retrieved from http://marketingland.com/ftc-puts-social-media-marketers-on-notice-with-updated-disclosure-guidelines-132017.

Best Buy Social Media Policy. October 22, 2020. https://forums.bestbuy.com/t5/Welcome-News/Best-Buy-Social-Media-Policy/td-p/20492.

Burkhalter, J.N., N.T. Wood, and S. Tryce. 2014. "Clear, Conspicuous, and Concise: Disclosures and Twitter Word-of-Mouth." *Business Horizons* 57, no. 3, pp. 319–28. doi:10.1016/j.bushor.2014.02.001.

Canning, N. October 01, 2019. "How to Legally Repost User-Generated Content on Instagram." https://later.com/blog/user-generated-content-rules/.

Castillo, M. 2014. "FTC After Deutsch L.A. Case: No, Agencies Can't Ask Staffers to Casually Tweet About Clients | Adweek." *AdWeek.* Retrieved from www.adweek.com/news/technology/ftc-no-agencies-cant-ask-staffers-casually-tweet-nice-things-about-clients-161755.

Coffee, P. 2016. "FTC Slams Lord & Taylor for Not Disclosing Paid Social Posts and Native Ads." *AdWeek.* Retrieved from www.adweek.com/news/advertising-branding/ftc-slams-lord-taylor-deceiving-customers-not-disclosing-its-native-ads-170229.

Davies, D. June 05, 2020. "Branded Content Tools on Instagram." https://business.instagram.com/a/brandedcontentexpansion.

Dingle, J.D. 1983. "FTC Policy Statement on Deception." www.ftc.gov/sites/default/files/attachments/training-materials/policy_deception.pdf.

Federal Trade Commission. 2008. "Guides Concerning the Use of Endorsements and Testimonials in Advertising—16 CFR Part 255." Retrieved from www.ecfr.gov/cgi-bin/text-idx?SID=745dabff622dbafa30e1ee08f7b4ad2a&mc=trueandnode=pt16.1.255andrgn=div5.

Federal Trade Commission. 2013. "Disclosures: How to Make Effective Disclosures in Digital Advertising." Federal Trade Commission. www.ftc.gov/tips-advice/business-center/guidance/com-disclosures-how-make-effective-disclosures-digital.

Federal Trade Commission. 2013a. "The FTC's Endorsement Guides: What People Are Asking." *The FTC's Endorsement Guides.* www.ftc.gov/tips-advice/business-center/guidance/ftcs-endorsement-guides-what-people-are-asking.

Federal Trade Commission. 2013b. "Dot Com Disclosures." Retrieved from www.ftc.gov/system/files/documents/plain-language/bus41-dot-com-disclosures-information-about-online-advertising.pdf.

Federal Trade Commission. 2015. "The FTC's Endorsement Guides: What People Are Asking." Retrieved from www.ftc.gov/tips-advice/business-center/guidance/ftcs-endorsement-guides-what-people-are-asking#when.

Federal Trade Commission. 2016a. "What We Do | Federal Trade Commission." Retrieved from www.ftc.gov/about-ftc/what-we-do.

Federal Trade Commission. 2016b. "Truth in Advertising | Federal Trade Commission." Retrieved from www.ftc.gov/news-events/media-resources/truth-advertising.

Federal Trade Commission. 2016c. "Lord & Taylor Settles FTC Charges It Deceived Consumers Through Paid Article in an Online Fashion Magazine and Paid Instagram Posts by 50 'Fashion Influencers'." FTC. Retrieved from www.ftc.gov/news-events/press-releases/2016/03/lord-taylor-settles-ftc-charges-it-deceived-consumers-through.

Federal Trade Commission. September 17, 2017. "The FTC's Endorsement Guides: What People Are Asking." www.ftc.gov/tips-advice/business-center/guidance/ftcs-endorsement-guides-what-people-are-asking.

"Fox News, North Jersey Media Group End Lawsuits Through Settlement." 2016. www.lawyerherald.com/articles/34360/20160217/fox-news-north-jersey-media-group-end-lawsuits-through-settlement.htm.

"F.T.C v. Transnet Wireless Corp", 506 F. Supp. 2d 1247, 1266. (S.D. Fla. 2007). Retrieved from www.leagle.com/decision/20071753506FSupp2d1247_11664/F.T.C.%20 v.%20TRANSNET%20WIRELESS%20CORP.

Hootsuite University. 2013. *Securing Your Organization in the Social Era With Charlene Li*. Hootsuite. Retrieved from https://learn.hootsuite.com.

Karp, H. 2017. "At Up to $250,000 a Ticket, Island Music Festival Woos Wealthy to Stay Afloat." *The Wall Street Journal*. www.wsj.com/articles/fyre-festival-organizers-push-to-keep-it-from-fizzling-1491130804.

Lagu, T., E.J. Kaufman, D.A. Asch, and K. Armstrong. 2008. "Content of Weblogs Written by Health Professionals." *Journal of General Internal Medicine* 23, no. 10, pp. 1642–46. doi:10.1007/s11606-008-0726-6.

Mann, R. October 2014. "Influential Instagrammers Part of New Underground Luxury Barter Economy." *AdWeek*. Retrieved from www.adweek.com/news/advertising-branding/inside-instagram-s-secret-barter-economy-160905.

Murabayashi, A. 2015. "Did I Just Give My #Permission? Hashtag Consent for Photo Usage Is Trending." *PetaPixel*. Retrieved from http://petapixel.com/2015/09/22/did-i-just-give-my-permission-hashtag-consent-for-photo-usage/.

Olya, G. August 23, 2021. "These Stars Get Paid Obscene Amounts of Money to Post One Picture." www.gobankingrates.com/net-worth/celebrities/these-stars-get-paid-obscene-amounts-of-money-to-post-one-picture/.

Petty, R.D. and J. Andrews. 2008. "Covert Marketing Unmasked: A Legal and Regulatory Guide for Practices That Mask Marketing Messages." *Journal of Public Policy & Marketing* 27, no. 1, pp. 7–18. doi:10.1509/jppm.27.1.7.

Roberts, J. 2016. "FTC Blasts Warner Bros Over Stealth Social Media Campaign." *Fortune*. Retrieved from http://fortune.com/2016/07/11/warner-bros-social-media/.

Sass, E. 2017. "Fyre Social Influencers Sued for Fraud 05/08/2017." *MediaPost*. www.mediapost.com/publications/article/300657/fyre-social-influencers-sued-for-fraud.html.

Smith, G. and L.L.P. Russell. 2016. "Social Media Marketing: The 411 on Legal Risk and Liability." Retrieved from www.sgrlaw.com/resources/trust_the_leaders/leaders_issues/ttl28/1597/ (accessed July 02, 2016).

The Coca-Cola Company. 2016a. "Mission, Vision & Values." Retrieved from www.coca-colacompany.com/our-company/mission-vision-values (accessed July 01, 2016).

The Coca-Cola Company. 2016b. "Social Media Principles." Retrieved from www.coca-colacompany.com/stories/online-social-media-principles.

The Fashion Law. May 22, 2019. "Your Doctors Might Be Running Afoul of Federal Law With Their Social Media Posts." www.thefashionlaw.com/?s=Your+Doctors+Might+Be+Running+Afoul+of+Federal+Law+With+Their+Social+Media+Post.

Thomas, K. May 15, 2019. "A Rival to Botox Invites Doctors to Party in Cancun, With Fireworks, Confetti and Social Media Posts." *The New York Times*.

Tung, E. 2014. "How to Write a Social Media Policy to Empower Employees." Social Media Examiner. Retrieved from www.socialmediaexaminer.com/write-a-social-media-policy/.

Wal-Mart Stores, Inc. 2016. "Walmart Policies and Guidelines." http://corporate.walmart.com/policies.

Williams, R. March 09, 2020. "FTC Fines Detox Tea Company $1M Over Instagram Ads." www.marketingdive.com/news/ftc-fines-detox-tea-company-1m-over-instagram-ads/573703/.

WOMMA. 2012. "Social Marketing Disclosure Guide." Retrieved from www.smartbrief.com/hosted/womma_1783/SMDisclosureGuide-Final.pdf.

WOMMA. 2014. "Ethical Word of Mouth Marketing Disclosure Best Practices in Today's Regulatory Environment." *Ethical Word of Mouth Marketing Disclosure Best Practices in Today's Regulatory Environment*.

Wouk, K. 2016. "Rihanna Sells Out $9000 Dolce & Gabanna Headphones." *Digital Trends*. Retrieved from www.digitaltrends.com/music/rihanna-sells-out-9000-dollar-dolce-gabanna-headphones/.

Zara, C. 2015. "Fox News, Jeanie Pirro Facebook Lawsuit Could Change Copyright Landscape on Social Media." *International Business Times*. Retrieved from www.ibtimes.com/fox-news-jeanie-pirro-facebook-lawsuit-could-change-copyright-landscape-social-media-1865246.

About the Authors

Natalie T. Wood, PhD, is an associate dean and professor of marketing at Saint Joseph's University. Her work in social media focuses on word of mouth, advertising, and influencer marketing. She is a coauthor of *Virtual Social Identity and Consumer Behavior and Maximizing Commerce and Marketing Strategies through Micro-Blogging.*

Caroline K. Muñoz, PhD, is a professor of marketing at the University of North Georgia. Her research explores marketing pedagogy and political marketing in visually oriented social media platforms.

Index

Account issues, 188
Account ownership, 188
Account status, 186–187
Acronyms, 96–97
Advocates, 173–175
Airtable, 77–78
Altruists, 41
Amplified word of mouth, 7
Audience, 11
Authority, 143–144

Blogs, 135
Boomerangs, 41
Brand advocates, 137
Brand ambassadors, 151
Brand awareness, 20, 77
Brand voice, 68–71, 188–189
Branson, R., 130
Business-to-business (B2B) market, 75–78, 96
Business-to-customer (B2C) market, 77

Call-to-action, 99–100
Campaign, 128
Careerists, 41
Celebrities, 151, 155–156
Clear and conspicuous disclosures, 162–165
Coca-Cola Company, 1–2, 85–86, 181, 182
Co-creation, 14
Collaborative word of mouth, 7
Commitment, 145–147
Communication, 12, 13
Company-generated communication, 17
Competition, 59–60
Compliance, 187
Connectors, 41

Consistency, 145–147
Consumer base, 58–59
Consumer content, 16
Consumer feedback, 5
Consumer influencers, 137–138
Consumer reviews, 11, 19
Consumer satisfaction, 21
Content, 128
Content marketing, 83–84
Copyright, 193–194
Creative strategies, 94–95
Crocs, 193
C-suite, 129–131
Customer services, 71–73

Deception, 158
Disclosure, 176–179

Earned media, 6
Electronic word of mouth (eWOM), 8–11
Emotional arousal, 91–93
Emotional capital, 130
Employee advocates, 131–137
Employee endorsements, 175–176
Employee engagement, 61–62
Endorsers, 173–174
Everyday consumers, 22, 85, 137, 148
eWOM. *See* Electronic word of mouth
Executive buy-in and support, 60–61
Explicit sharing, 39
External influencers, 122

Facebook, 134
Federal Trade Commission (FTC)
  commonly asked questions, 172–179
  definition of, 157–158
  disclosure, 161

endorsement guidelines for clear and conspicuous disclosures, 162–165
industry regulations, 168–169
material connections, 159–160
method of disclosure, 165–168
responsibilities, 161–162
FTC. *See* Federal Trade Commission
Full URL, 129

Hashtags, 101–102
Hipsters, 41

IBM, 76
Image attributes, 110–112
Implicit sharing, 39
Independence, 187
Influencers, 173–175
 consumer, 137–138
 employee advocates, 131–137
 external, 122
 identifying and hiring, 124–126
 internal, 129–131
 Klear's influencer informational guidelines, 126–127
 launch and build, 136–137
 macro, 123
 mega, 122–123
 micro, 123–124
 mid-tier, 123
 nano, 124
 overview of, 121
 programs and compensation, 43, 126–127
 reach, 125
 relevance, 125
 resonance, 125–126
 risk, 125
 social media platforms, 133–135
Innovation, 64
Instagram, 134–135
Internal influencers, 129–131

Legal and regulatory issues, 23. *See also* Federal Trade Commission (FTC)
Length, 95–96

Liking, 148–149
LinkedIn, 134
Links, 100–101
Lord & Taylor, 156–157

Macro influencers, 123
Maersk Group, 76
Marketing
 communications, 65–67
 implications, 46–47
Medium, 128
Mega influencers, 122–123
Message valence, 91–93
Micro influencers, 123–124
Mid-tier influencers, 123
Musk, E., 130–131, 134

Nano influencers, 124
New York Times, 41

Official accounts, 186
Online media, 6
Organic word of mouth, 7
Owned media, 6

Paid media, 6
Paid social influencers, 122–124
Personal accounts, 11
Persuasion principles
 authority, 143–144
 commitment, 145–147
 consistency, 145–147
 liking, 148–149
 reciprocity, 141–143
 scarcity, 145
 social proof, 147
Pinterest, 30, 37, 40, 100, 105, 108–111
Policy statement, 186
Public information, 57–58

Quotes, 102

Reciprocity, 141–143
Regulations
 industry, 168–169
 laws and, 185

SAP. *See* Systems Applications and Products
Scalability, 13
Scarcity, 145
Selectives, 41
Shopify, 76
Shortened URL, 129
Slack, 76–77
Social B2B companies, 75–78
Social business
  definition of, 55
  overview of, 53–55
  in sWOM, 22
Social business maturity model
  brand voice, 68–71
  competition, 59–60
  consumer base, 58–59
  customer services, 71–73
  employee engagement, 61–62
  executive buy-in and support, 60–61
  humanizing brand, 67–68
  human resources, 64–65
  innovation, 64
  marketing communications, 65–67
  maturity phase, 74–75
  presentation of, 56
  public information, 57–58
  social connections, 58
  strategic insights and execution, 63–64
  transition phase, 61
  trial phase, 55, 57
Social connections, 58
Social consumer, 44–45
  accessing social media, 32–33
  definition of, 29–30
  description of, 30–32
  levels of engagement, 34–35
  social influencers, 43–44
  social listener, 35–38
  social sharers, 38–43
Social influence, 43, 141, 150
Social influencer, 43–44. *See also* Influencers
  examples, 156–157
  success, 127–129
Social listener, 35–38

Social media
  deception, 158
  employees on, 169–171
  engagement, 20
Social Media Advisory Board, 182–183
Social media engagement pyramid, 34–35
Social media policy
  company culture, 181–182
  copyright on, 193–194
  distributing feedback, 186
  drafting document, 186
  introducing, 191–192
  necessity of, 180
  periodic review, 192
  purpose of, 180–181
  research, 183–185
  Social Media Advisory Board, 182–183
Social media policy inclusions
  account issues, 188
  account ownership, 188
  account status, 186–187
  approved platforms, 186
  best practices, 189–191
  brand voice, 188–189
  legal issues, 188
  policy statement, 186
Social proof, 147
Social sharers, 38–43
Social word of mouth (sWOM)
  definition of, 10
  examples of, 20–21
  explanation of, 10–11
  importance of, 19–20
  scope of, 12
  typology of, 16
Source content, 128
Sour Patch Kids, 157
Storytelling
  content and, 88–91
  creative strategies, 94–95
  keys to successful, 86–88
  message valence and emotional arousal, 91–93
  overview of, 83–84
  in sWOM, 22

textual, 95
visual, 102–103
visual analytics and commerce, 108–109
Strong ties, 10
Structuring influencer programs, 126–127
sWOM. *See* Social word of mouth
Systems Applications and Products (SAP), 78–79

Teami, 156
Termination, 187
Terms, 128
Textual storytelling
  acronyms, 96–97
  call-to-action, 99–102
  hashtags, 101–102
  length, 95–96
  links, 100–101
  quotes, 102
  word choice, 97–99
Tourism Australia, social sharing
  authority, 150–151
  commitment, 151
  consistency, 151
  liking, 151–152
  overview of, 149–150
  reciprocity, 150
  social proof, 151
Traditional word of mouth, 6–8
Twitter, 133–134

Unofficial accounts, 187
Urchin Traffic Monitor (UTM), 128, 129
URL, 127–128
User descriptors, 12
UTM Tag Builder, 129

Viral marketing, 7
Visual analytics, 108–109
Visual commerce, 108–109
Visual storytelling
  not for options, 107–108
  photos and consumption practices, 105–106
  popularity, 104–105
  power of images, 103–104
  videos and other digital assets, 106–107

Weak ties, 9–10
WOM. *See* Word of mouth
WOMM. *See* Word of mouth marketing
WOMMA. *See* Word of Mouth Marketing Association
Word choice, 97–99
Word of mouth (WOM)
  electronic, 8–10
  importance of, 3–4
  organic, 7
  reasons for, 2–6
  social. *See* Social word of mouth marketing (sWOM)
  traditional, 6–8
Word of mouth marketing (WOMM), 2–6, 84
Word of Mouth Marketing Association (WOMMA), 3

YouTube, 5, 29–32, 35

OTHER TITLES IN THE DIGITAL AND SOCIAL MEDIA MARKETING AND ADVERTISING COLLECTION

Naresh Malhotra, Georgia Tech, Editor

- *Celebrity 2.0* by Stacy Landreth Grau
- *Cryptosocial* by Allen Taylor
- *Stand Out!!* by Brian McGurk
- *Super Sonic Logos* by David Allan
- *The Digital Marketing Landscape* by Jessica Rogers
- *Marketing in the Digital World* by Avinash Kapoor
- *Digital Marketing Management, Second Edition* by Debra Zahay
- *Make Your Nonprofit Social* by Lindsay Chambers, Jennifer Morehead, and Heather Sallee
- *Make Your Business Social* by Lindsay Chambers, Jennifer Morehead, and Heather Sallee
- *Social Media Marketing, Second Edition* by Emi Moriuchi
- *Tell Me About Yourself* by Stavros Papakonstantinidis

Concise and Applied Business Books

The Collection listed above is one of 30 business subject collections that Business Expert Press has grown to make BEP a premiere publisher of print and digital books. Our concise and applied books are for...

- Professionals and Practitioners
- Faculty who adopt our books for courses
- Librarians who know that BEP's Digital Libraries are a unique way to offer students ebooks to download, not restricted with any digital rights management
- Executive Training Course Leaders
- Business Seminar Organizers

Business Expert Press books are for anyone who needs to dig deeper on business ideas, goals, and solutions to everyday problems. Whether one print book, one ebook, or buying a digital library of 110 ebooks, we remain the affordable and smart way to be business smart. For more information, please visit www.businessexpertpress.com, or contact sales@businessexpertpress.com.

Printed in Poland
by Amazon Fulfillment
Poland Sp. z o.o., Wrocław